SMART SKETCH BOOK 9

Oogie Art's step-by-step guide to rendering hair in charcoal and pastel.

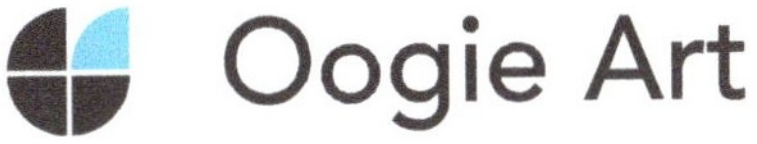

Oogie Art's SmartSketchbook™
An Expert's Guide to Hair Textures in Charcoal and Pastel
First Edition, Copyright © 2015

Produced and Edited by
Oogie Art
New York, NY

© Text
Oogie Art

© Photographs
Licensed under Oogie Art®

Directed by
Wook Choi

Assistant Directed by
Clara Lu

Drawings by
Jee Hwang

Tips by
Wook Choi

Published and Distributed by
Oogie Publishing House
New York, NY
www.oogiepublishinghouse.com
(212) 714-1011

ISBN 978-0-9968216-0-5
Printed in the United States

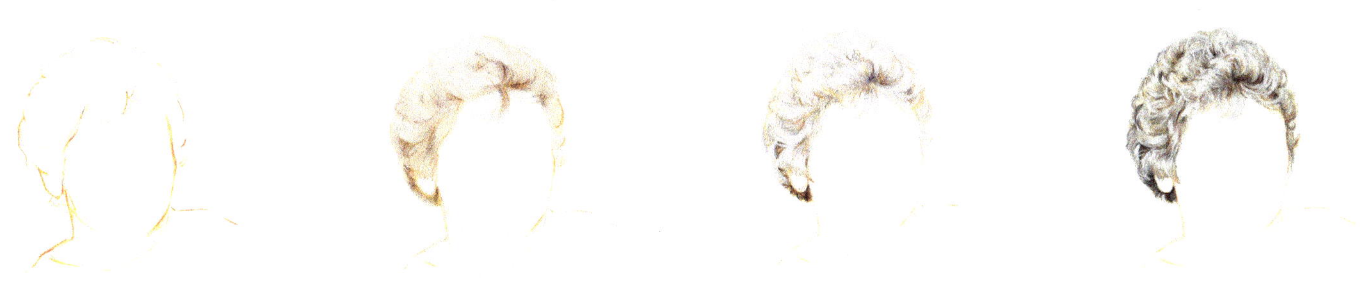

CONTENTS

Introduction to Hair Textures

Drawing hair can be daunting at first. Simplifying the highlights and shadows the hair makes into shapes will make things easier. A common mistake is forgetting what direction your light is coming from. Hair will be affected by the shape of the skull underneath. Keep this in mind so that your highlights reflect the volume of the head, with shadows on the same side as the shadows of the face. Do not make your drawing overly complicated with texture, this will draw attention away from your face and the other details of your drawing.

Hair often clumps together to form locks. Simplifying the shapes of these locks will make your job a lot easier. Once you have the general shape, you can add details and texture to your hair. Remember to keep your strokes in the same direction as your hair to help create realistic texture. Drawing hair is creating the illusion of individual strands, not drawing every single one.

What you'll need

- Vine charcoal
- Compressed charcoal
- Eraser
- Soft pastel and pastel pencils

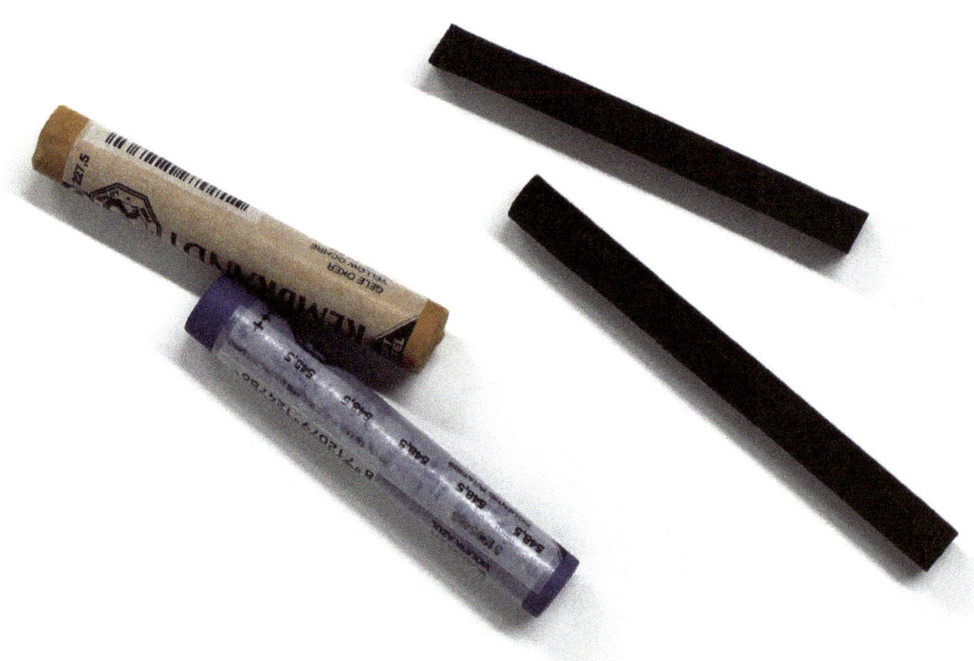

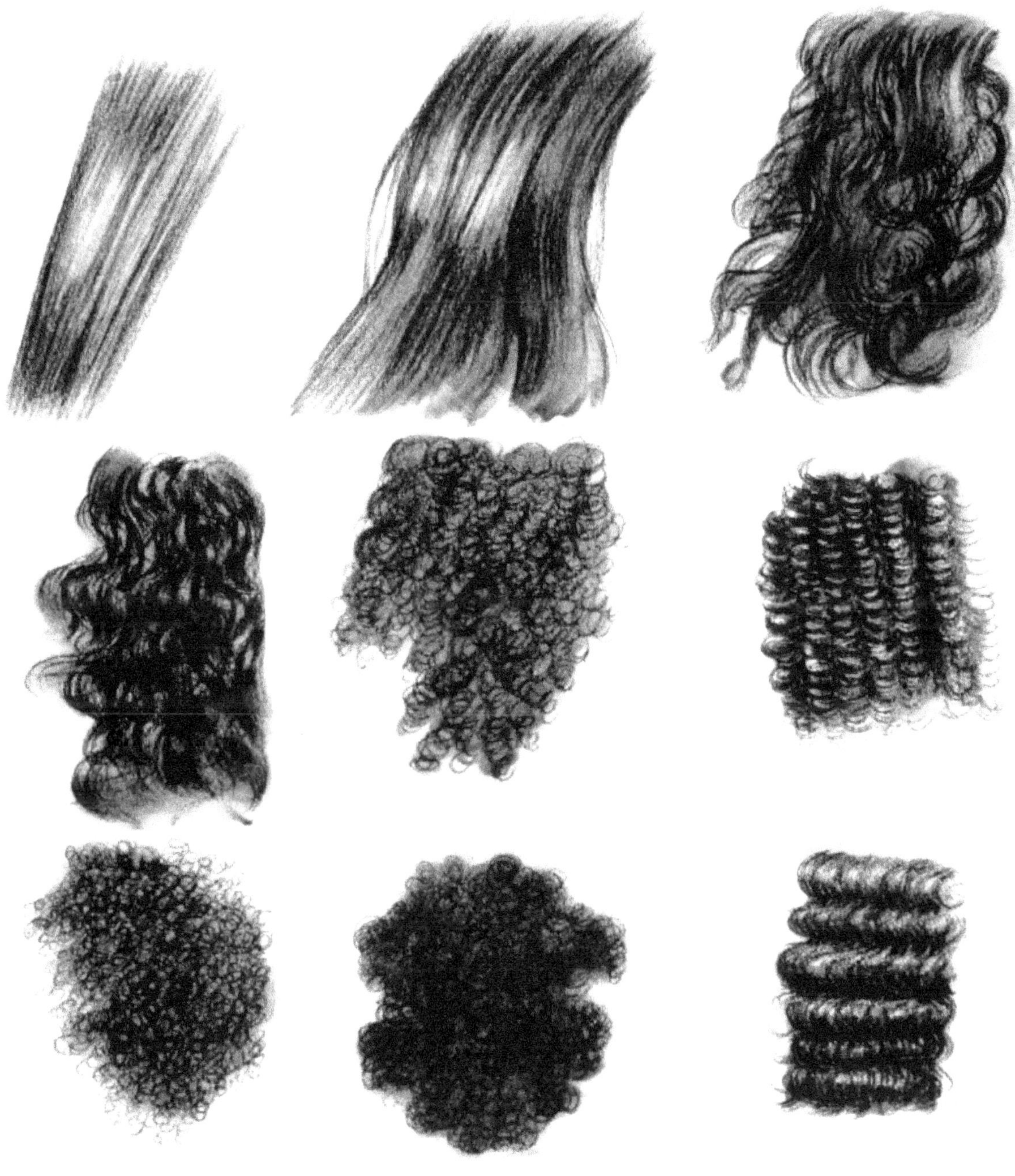

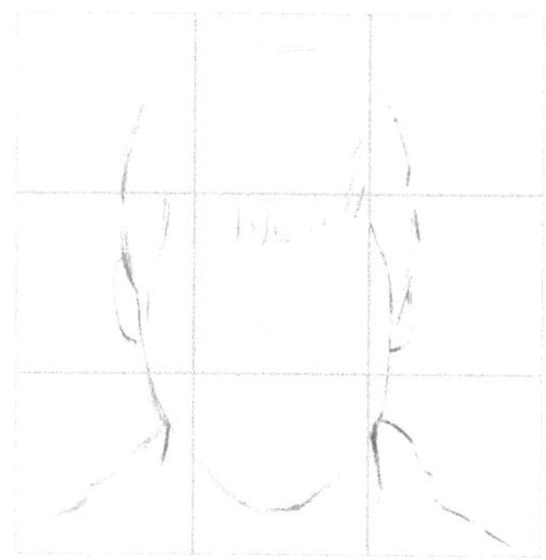
Begin by creating a general outline of the hair and face using vine charcoal.

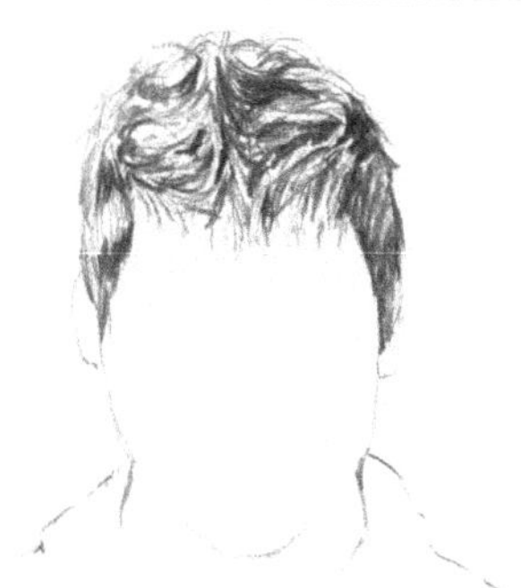
Generally block in the direction of the hair using rough marks.

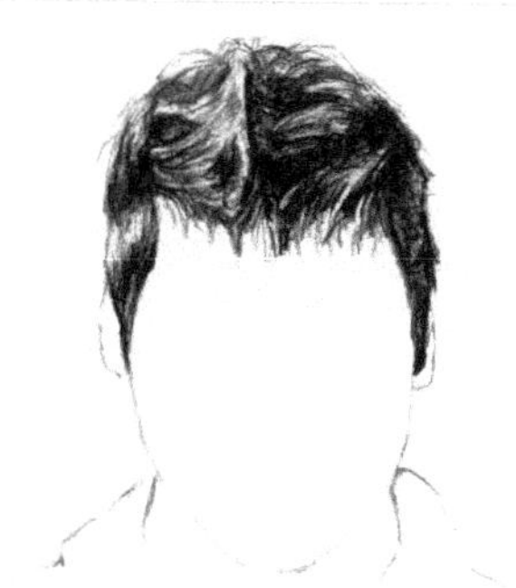
Continue to render the volume of the hair paying attention to the overal volume and introducing compressed charcoal.

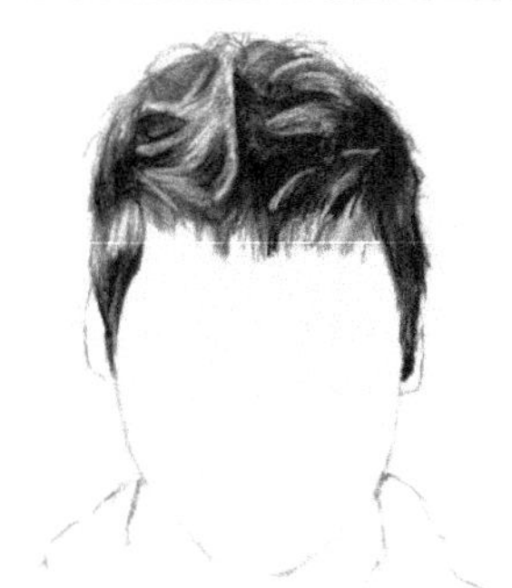
Soften your lines by blending and shading, then render hair lines using the sharp edge of an eraser.

Notice that the hairs on one side of the hair are lighter, this is there the light source is coming from.

At the end, create the textures of the hair using the sharp edge of an eraser.

Pay attention to the directions of the hair.

Focus on the general structure of the hair.

Use short strokes because the hair is short.

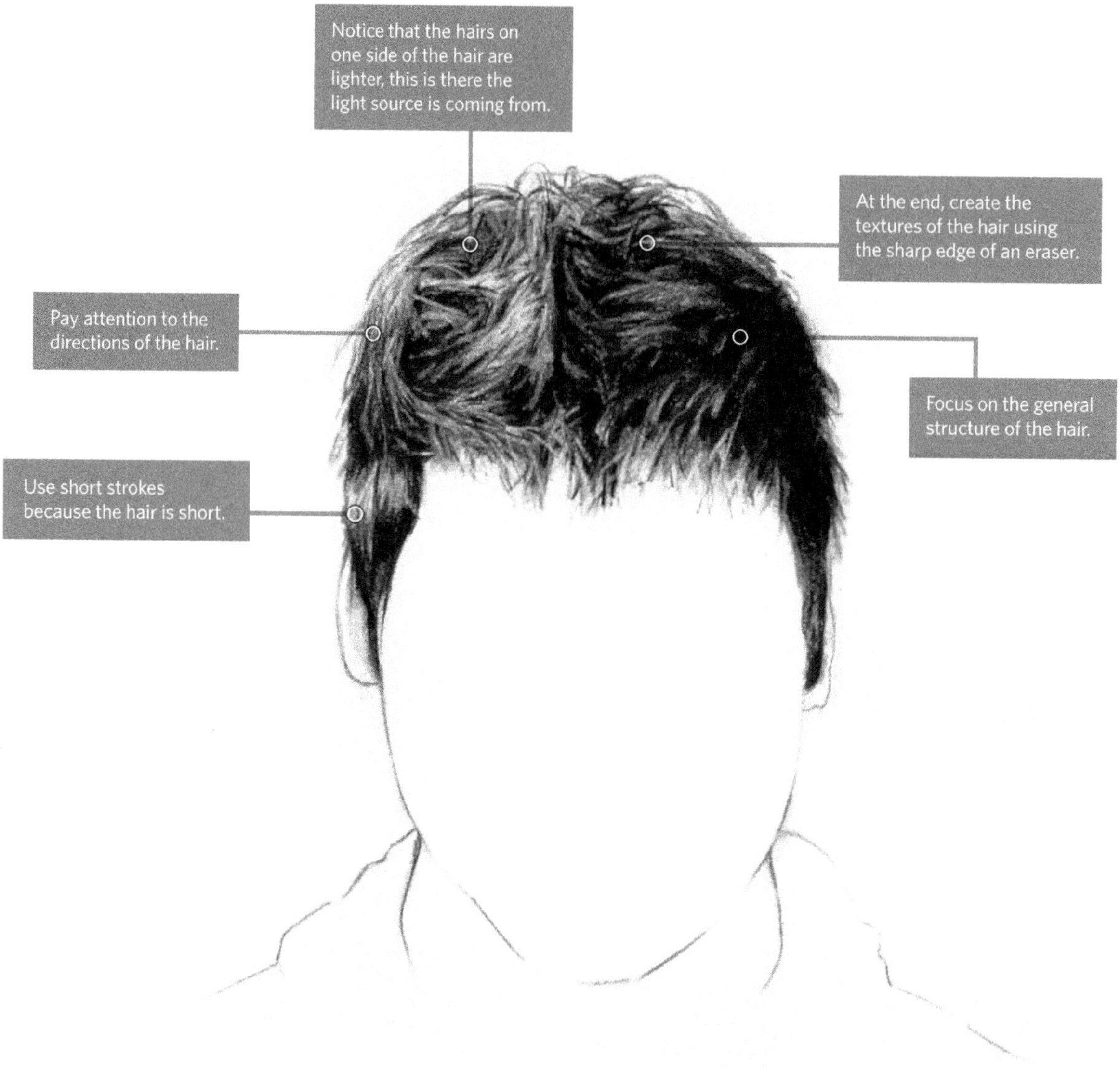

Now try drawing the short dark hair in charcoal.

Once you lay out the basic shape of the hair, start blocking in the dark shadows. Follow the direction of the hair with your marks; this makes for a more realistic appearance. After smoothing out the transitions in value, put down hard lines to show individual strands of hair, adding stray hairs around the edge of the head is a nice detail.

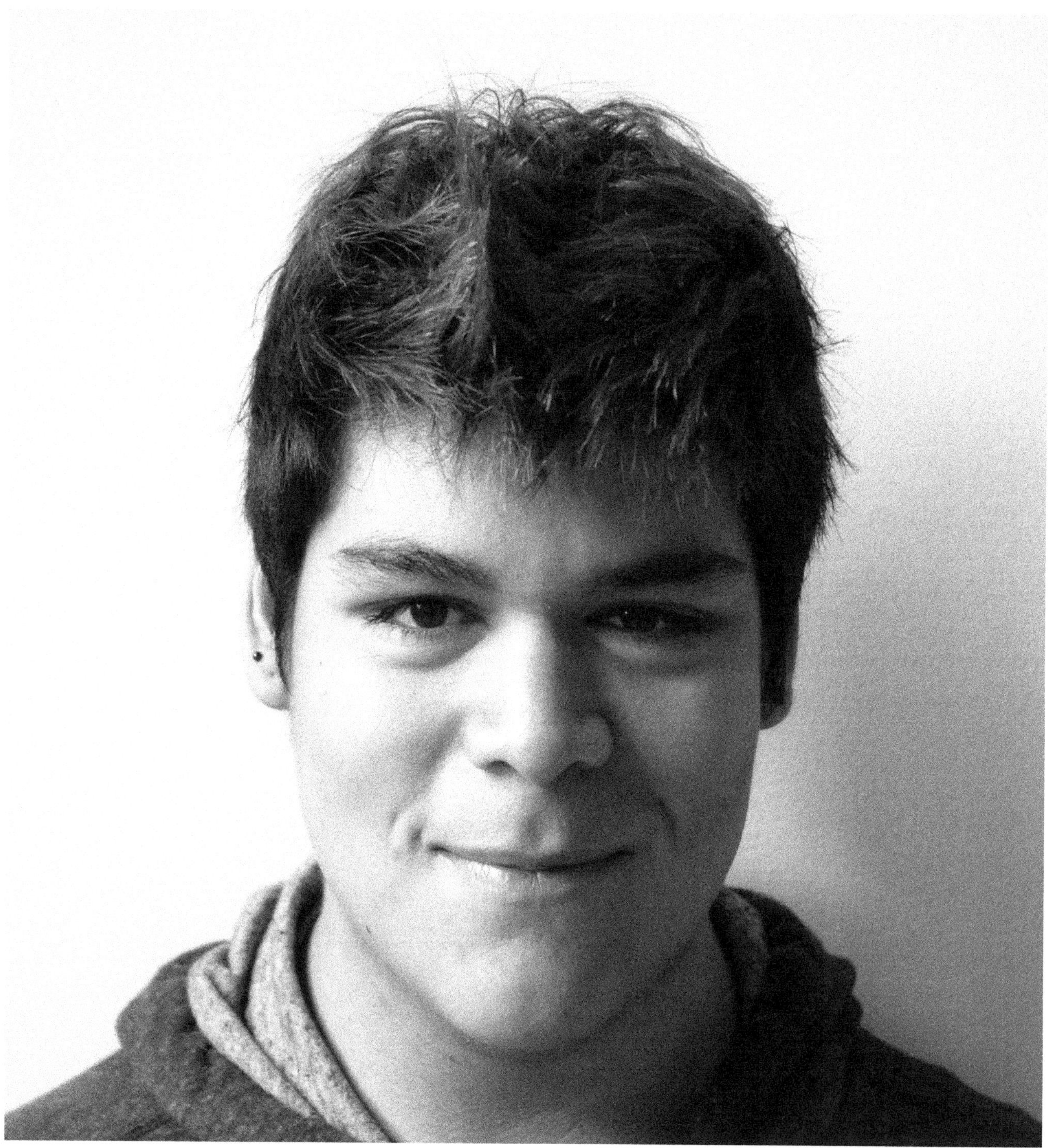

Now try drawing the short dark hair without using the grid.

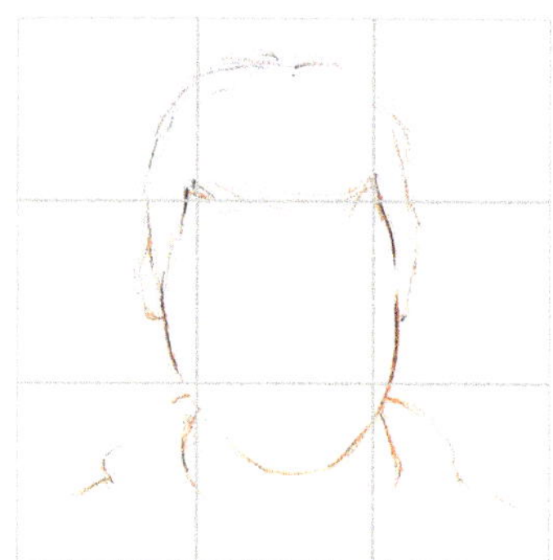

Begin by creating a general outline of the hair and face using a light brown pastel, such as raw sienna.

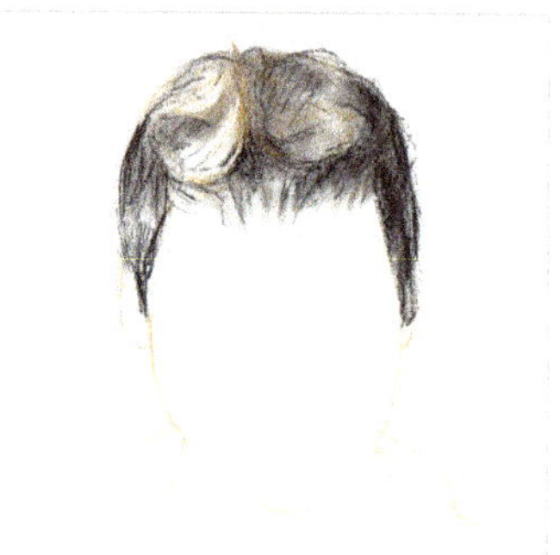

Generally block in the direction of the hair using rough marks of vine charcoal and raw umber.

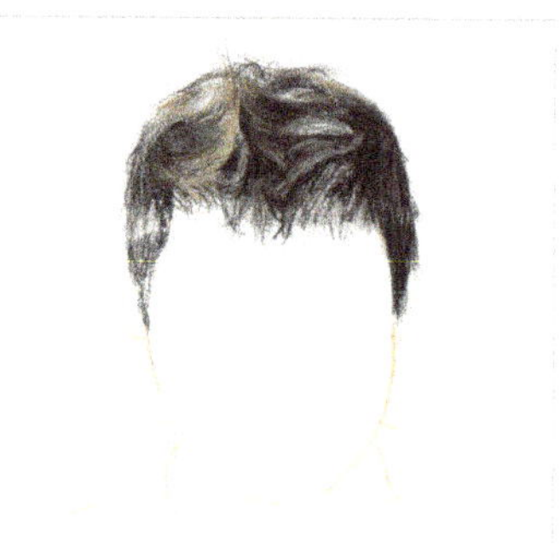

Continue to render the volume of the hair paying attention to the overal volume and introducing different browns mixed with charcoal.

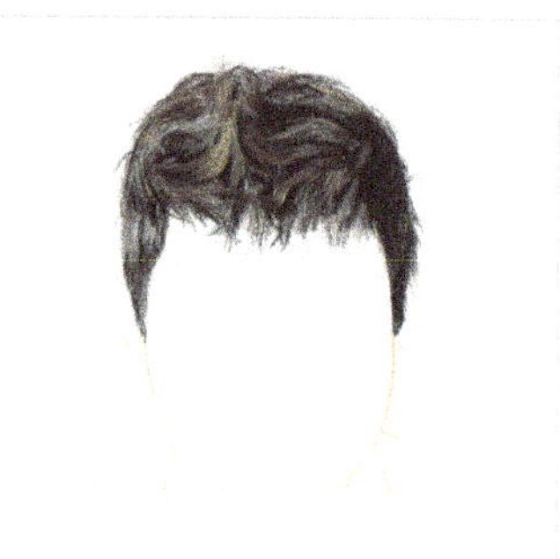

Soften your lines by blending and shading, then render hair lines using the sharp edge of an eraser. Use some yellows and greens to create the illusion of dyed hair.

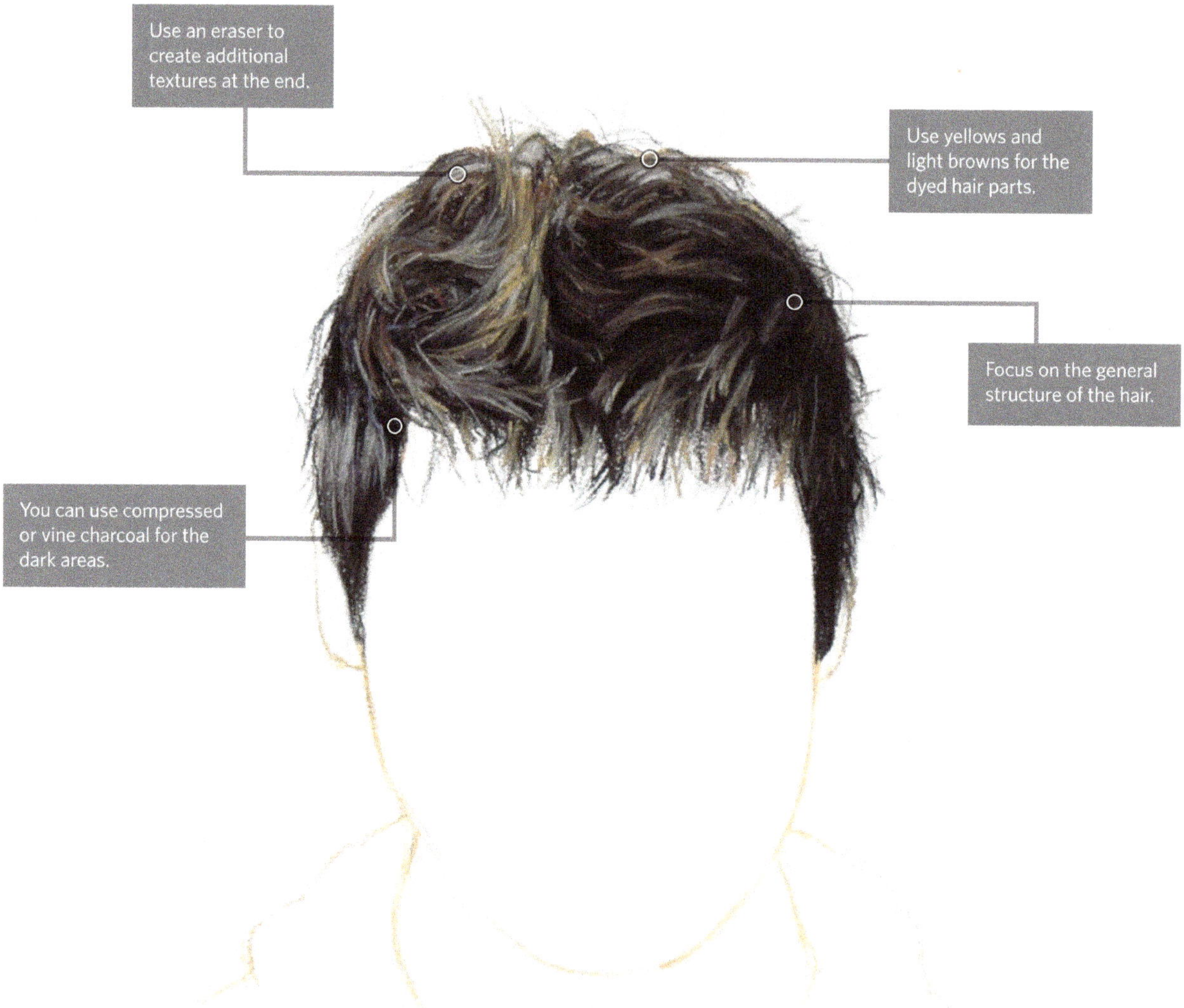

Use an eraser to create additional textures at the end.

Use yellows and light browns for the dyed hair parts.

Focus on the general structure of the hair.

You can use compressed or vine charcoal for the dark areas.

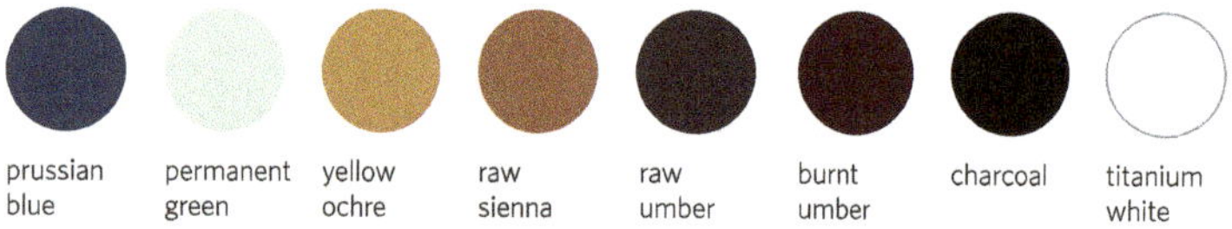

prussian blue

permanent green

yellow ochre

raw sienna

raw umber

burnt umber

charcoal

titanium white

Now try drawing the short dark hair in pastels.

After laying out the basic shape of the hair, start blocking in your values. Pay attention to the color of the hair. For example, the highlights in blonde or light brown hair will have yellow and even some red tones. High lights in dark brown or black hair will be mostly blue.

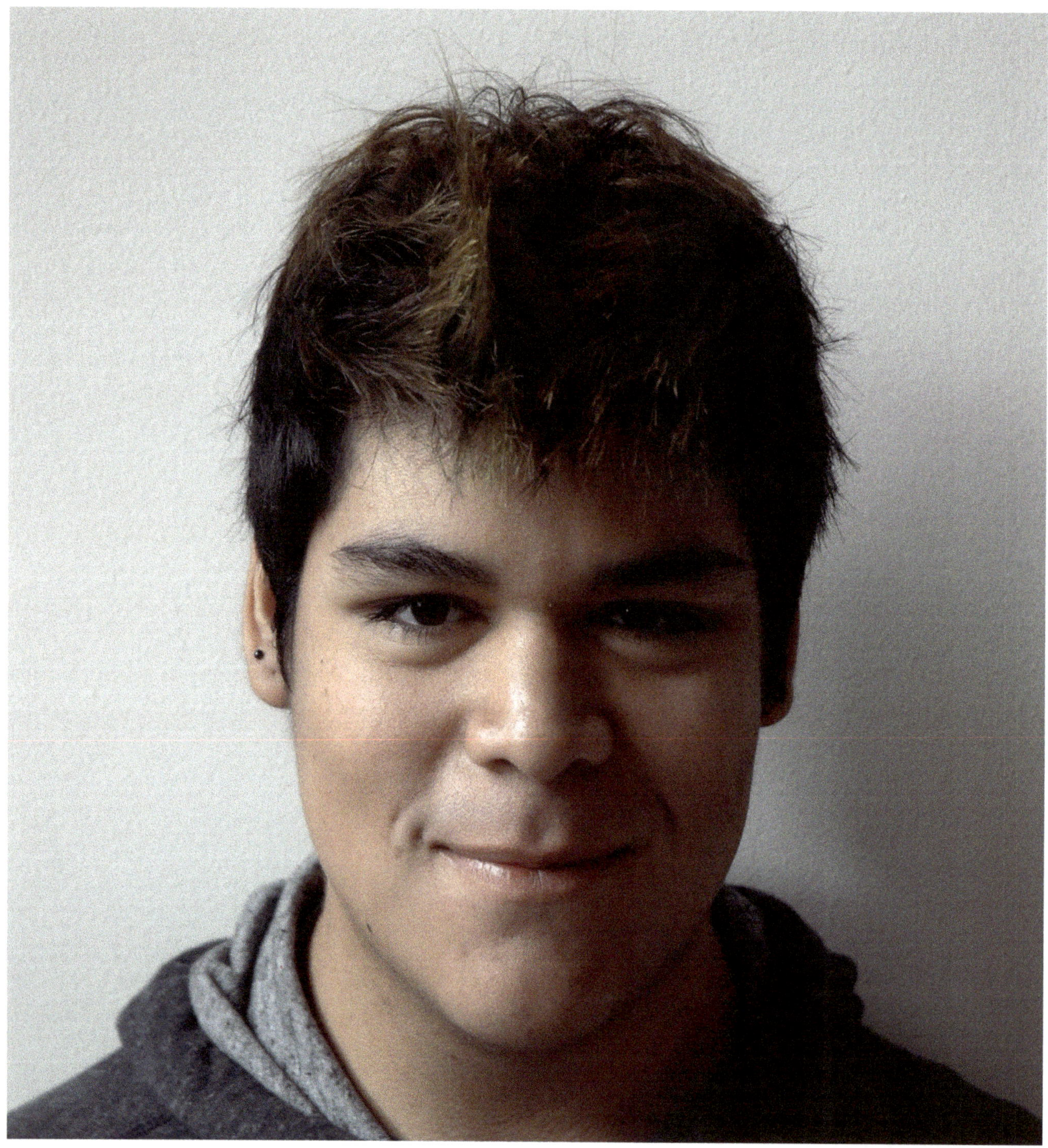

Now try drawing the short dark hair in pastel without using the grid.

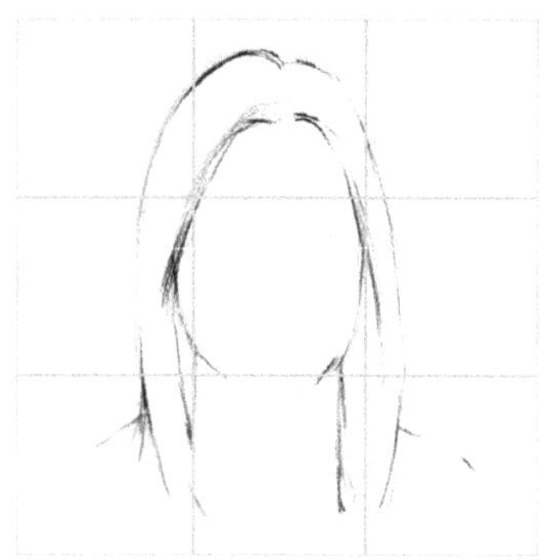

Begin by creating a general outline of the hair and face.

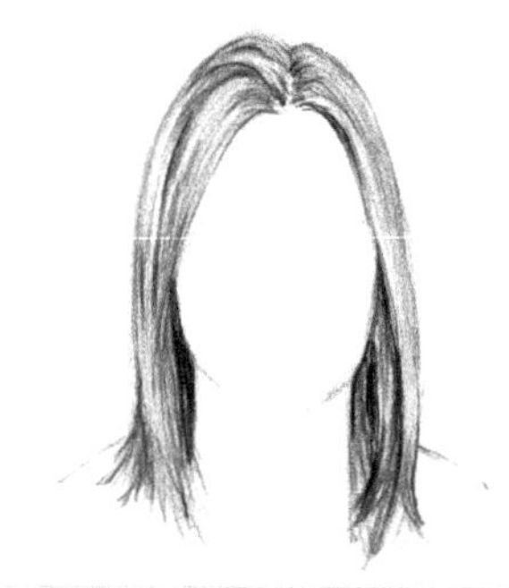

Generally block in the direction of the hair using rough marks.

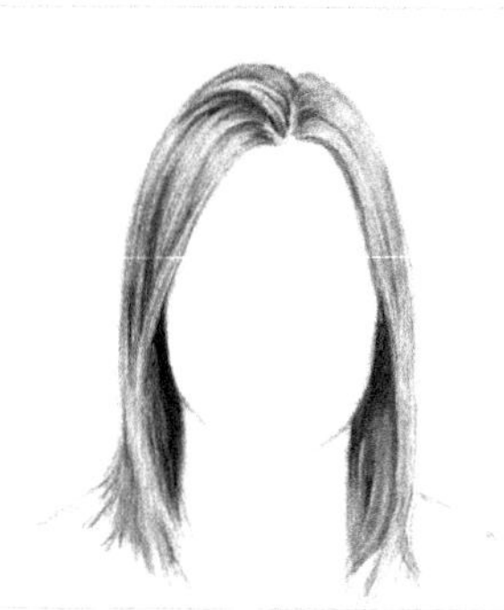

Continue to render the volume of the hair paying attention to the overal volume and introducing compressed charcoal.

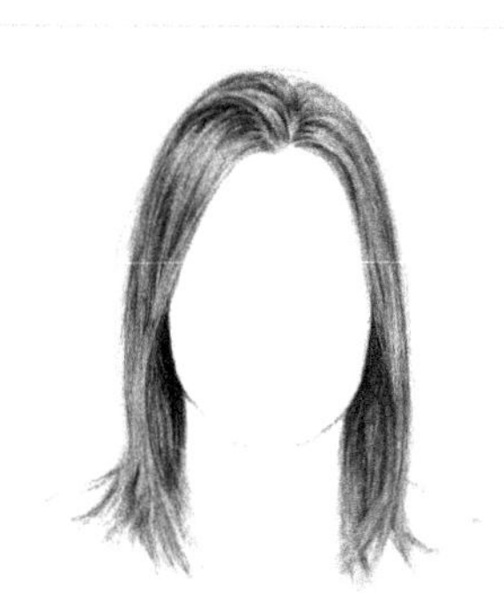

Soften your lines by blending and shading, then render hair lines using the sharp edge of an eraser.

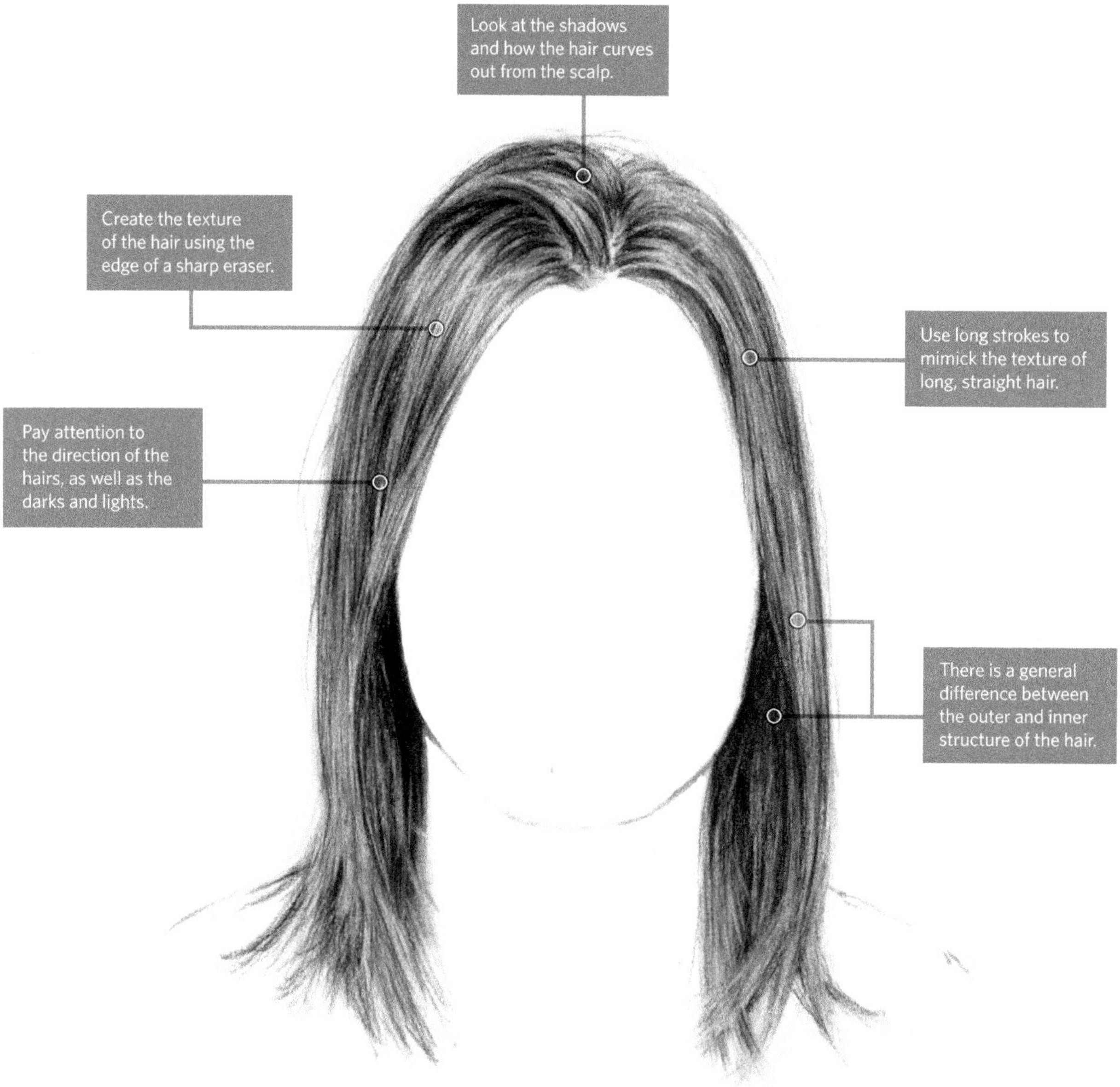

Look at the shadows and how the hair curves out from the scalp.

Create the texture of the hair using the edge of a sharp eraser.

Use long strokes to mimick the texture of long, straight hair.

Pay attention to the direction of the hairs, as well as the darks and lights.

There is a general difference between the outer and inner structure of the hair.

Now try drawing the short blonde hair in charcoal.

It is very important that your marks follow the direction of the hair. Long even strokes will make hair look smooth and straight. Emphasize the shadows by making thicker darker marks. Take your eraser and bring back highlights, which usually follow the curves in hair where it catches light.

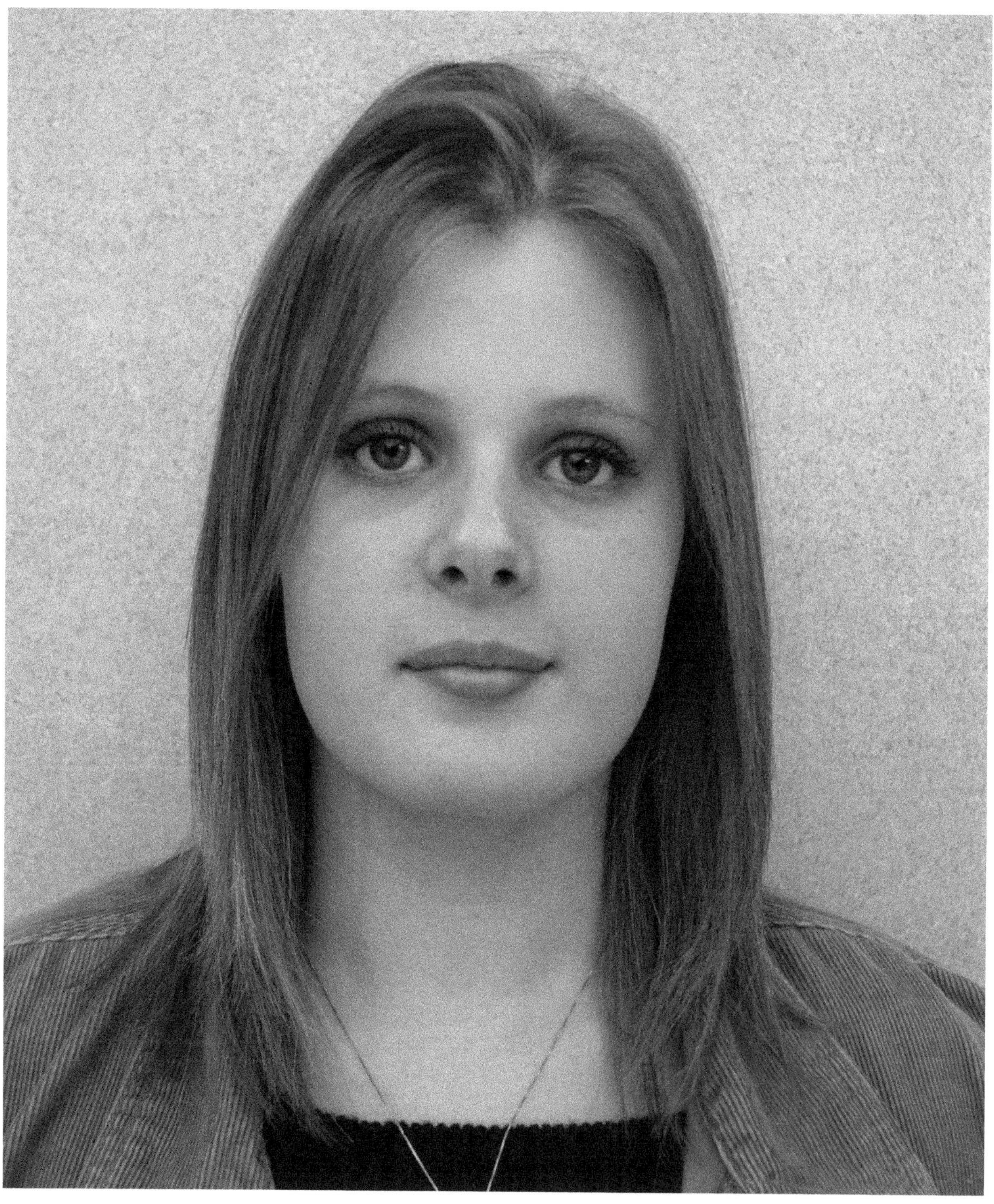

SHORT BLONDE HAIR IN CHARCOAL: PRACTICE II

Now try drawing the short blonde hair in charcoal without using the grid.

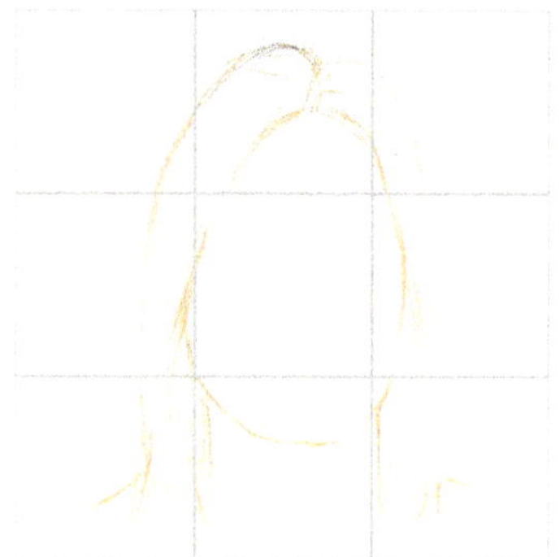

Begin by creating a general outline of the hair and face using a light brown pastel, such as yellow ochre.

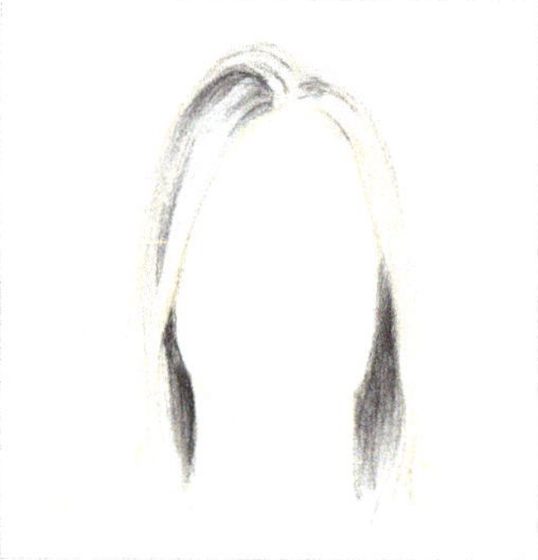

Generally block in the direction of the hair using rough marks of vine charcoal and yellow ochre.

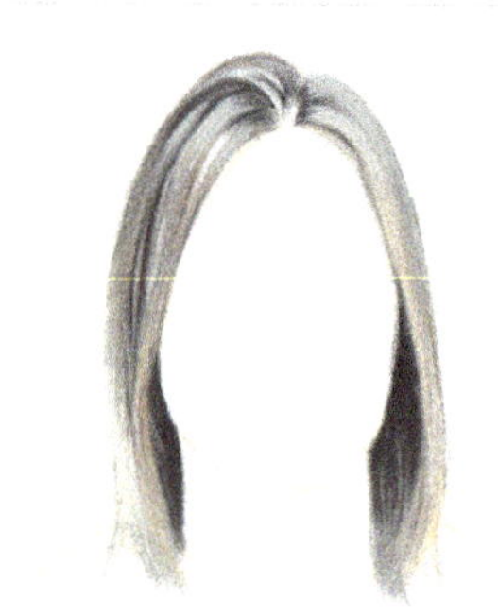

Continue to render the volume of the hair paying attention to the overal volume and introducing different light browns and yellows mixed with vine charcoal.

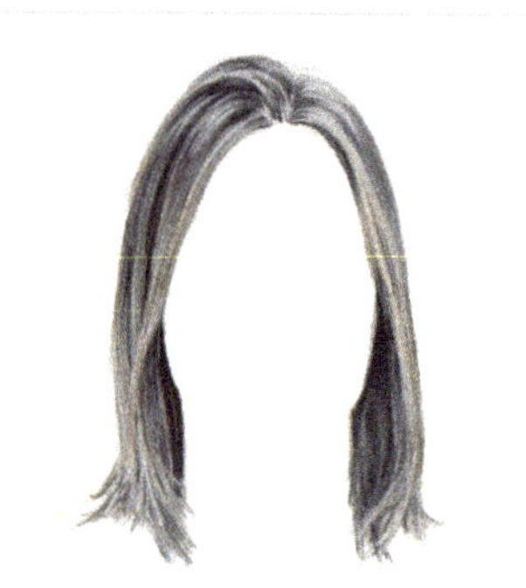

Soften your lines by blending and shading, then render hair lines using the sharp edge of an eraser. Use some light grays and yellows to create the illusion of blonde hair.

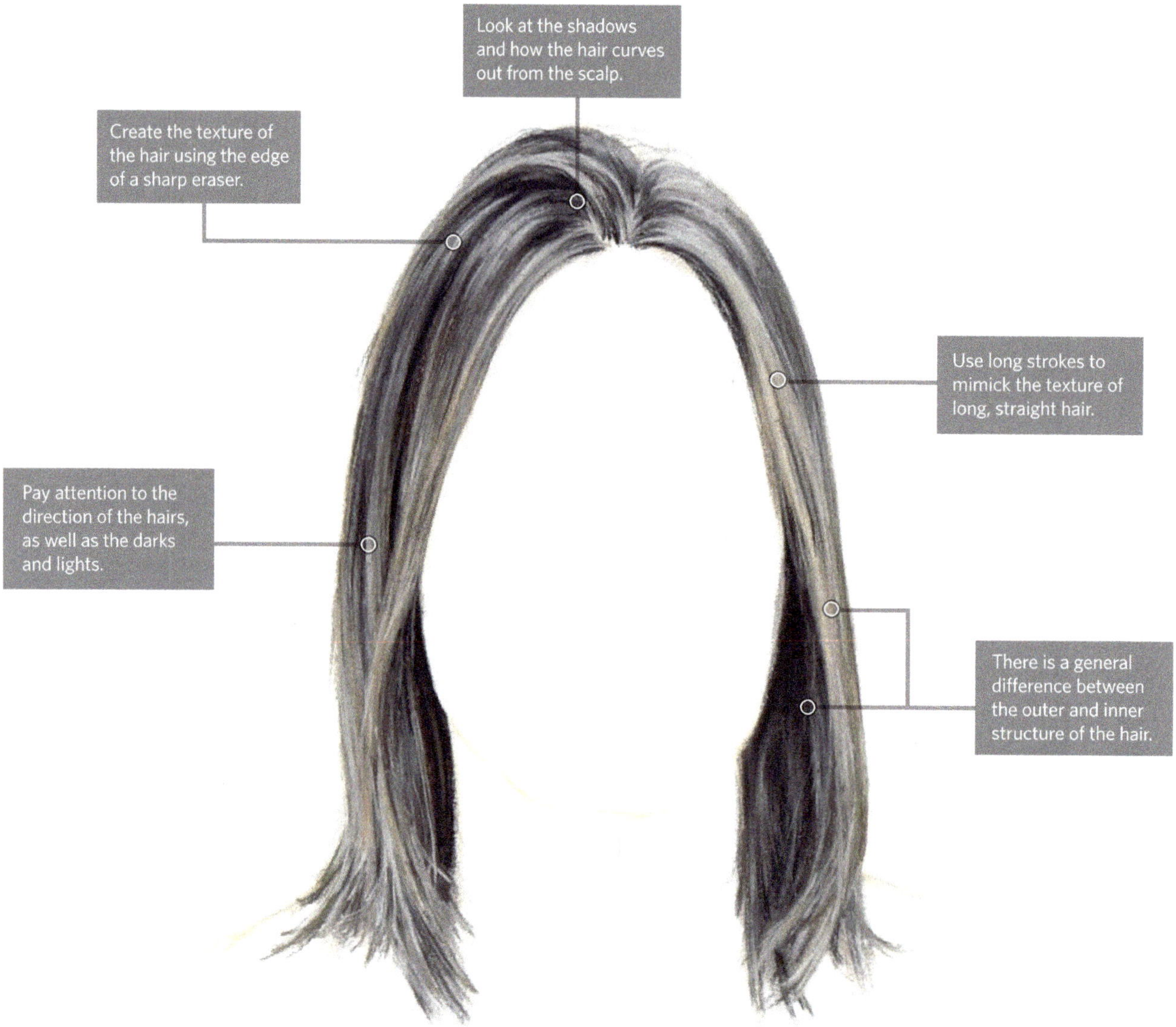

Look at the shadows and how the hair curves out from the scalp.

Create the texture of the hair using the edge of a sharp eraser.

Use long strokes to mimick the texture of long, straight hair.

Pay attention to the direction of the hairs, as well as the darks and lights.

There is a general difference between the outer and inner structure of the hair.

prussian blue | permanent green | yellow ochre | raw umber | burnt umber | charcoal | green gray | green gray | titanium white

Now try drawing the short blonde hair in pastels.

Although blonde hair appears light, it is important for your drawing to contain a wide range of values from dark to light. Choose lighter colors that contain yellows, light grays, and browns for your highlights and midtones. Dark brown should still be used in your dark shadows.

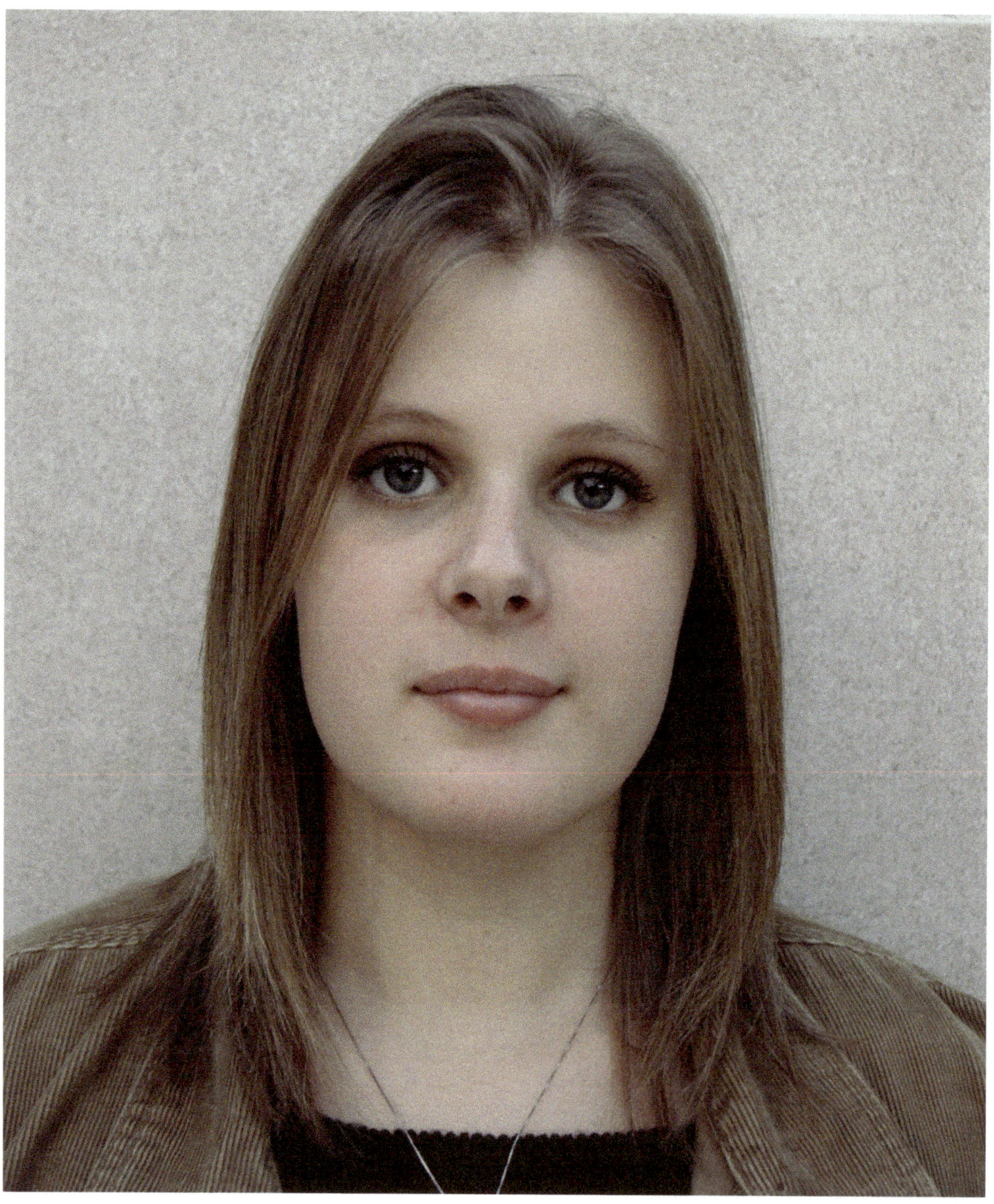

Now try drawing the short blonde hair in pastels without using the grid.

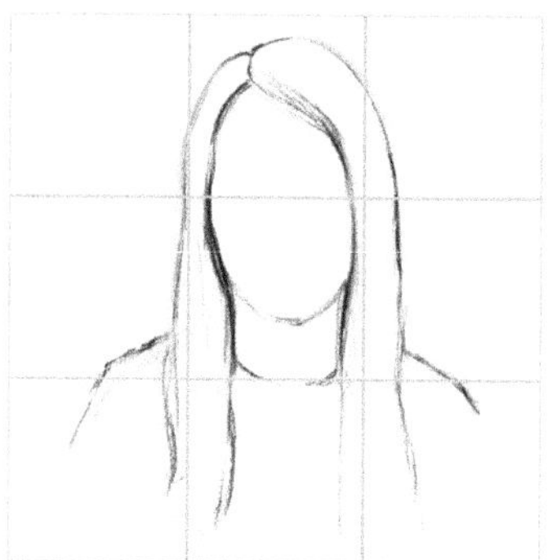

Begin by creating a general outline of the hair and face.

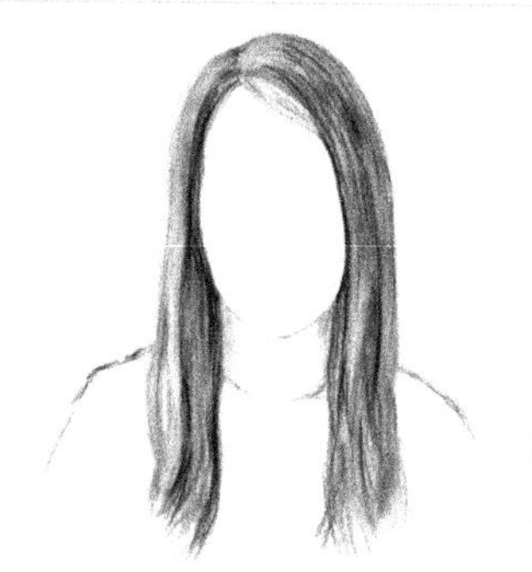

Generally block in the direction of the hair using rough marks.

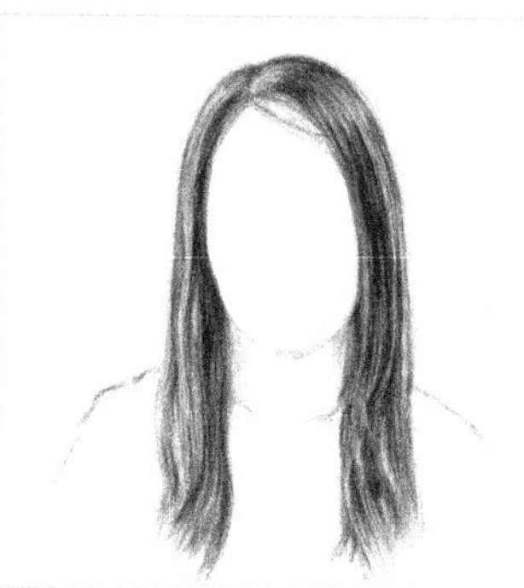

Continue to render the volume of the hair paying attention to the overal volume and introducing compressed charcoal.

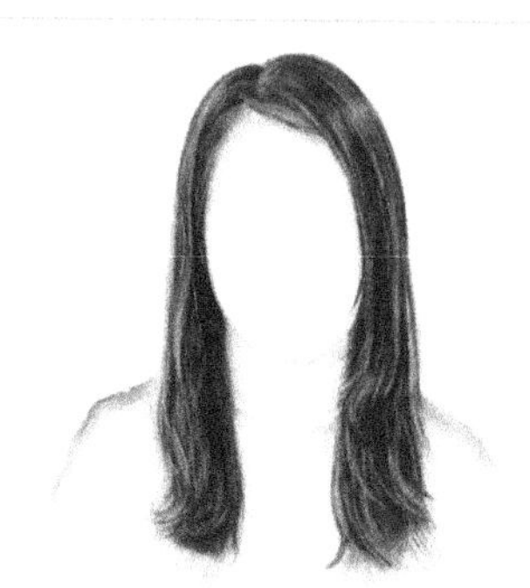

Soften your lines by blending and shading, then render hair lines using the sharp edge of an eraser.

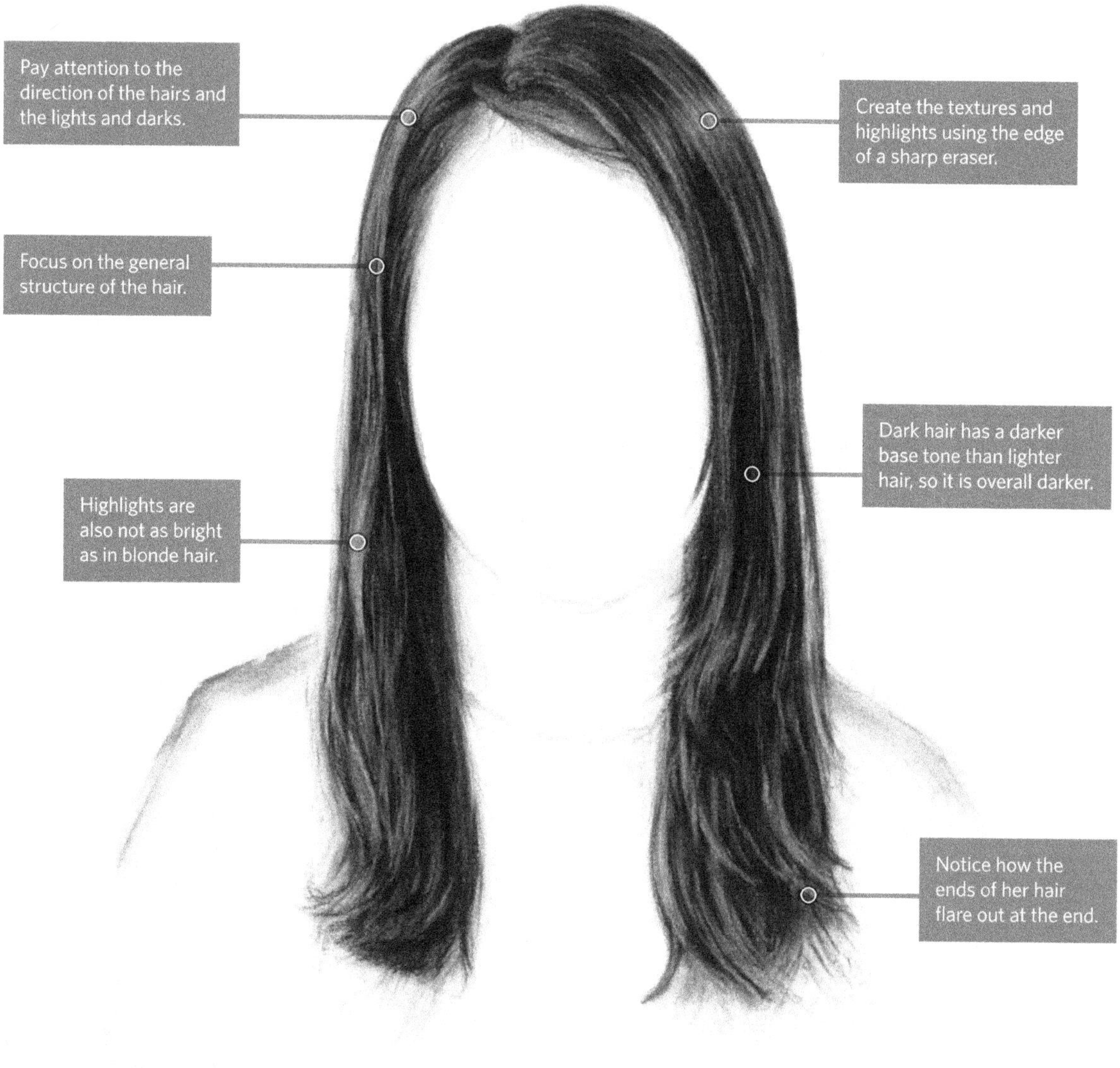

Pay attention to the direction of the hairs and the lights and darks.

Create the textures and highlights using the edge of a sharp eraser.

Focus on the general structure of the hair.

Dark hair has a darker base tone than lighter hair, so it is overall darker.

Highlights are also not as bright as in blonde hair.

Notice how the ends of her hair flare out at the end.

Now try drawing the long dark straight hair in charcoal yourself.

Once again, following the direction of the hair with your marks is very important. Dark hair will contain more shadow than midtone, but it is important to create volume with highlights. Once you have your darks laid in, take back your highlights (also following the direction of the hair) using your eraser.

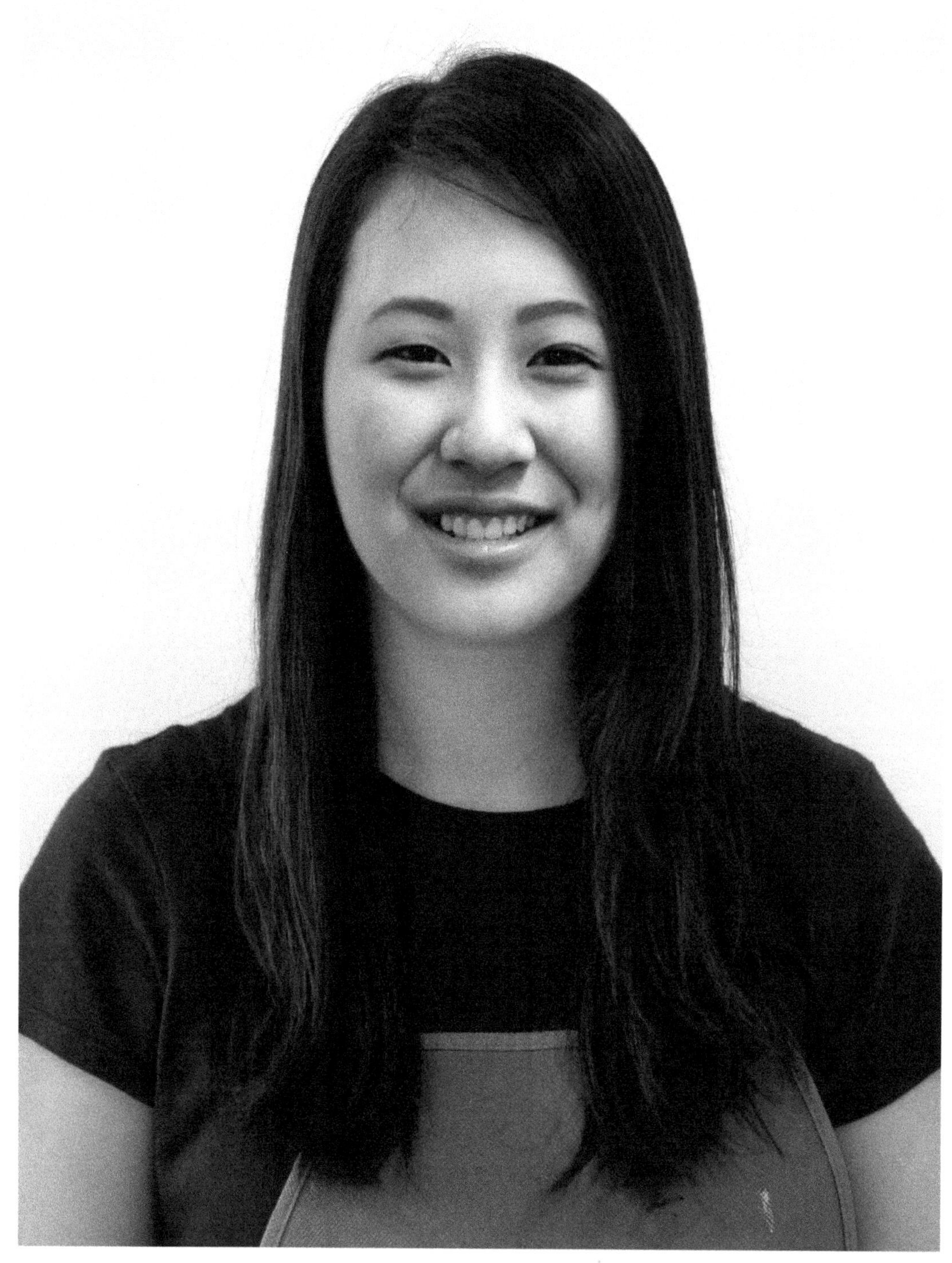

Now try drawing the long dark straight hair in charcoal yourself without the grid.

Begin by creating a general outline of the hair and face using a light brown pastel, such as raw sienna.

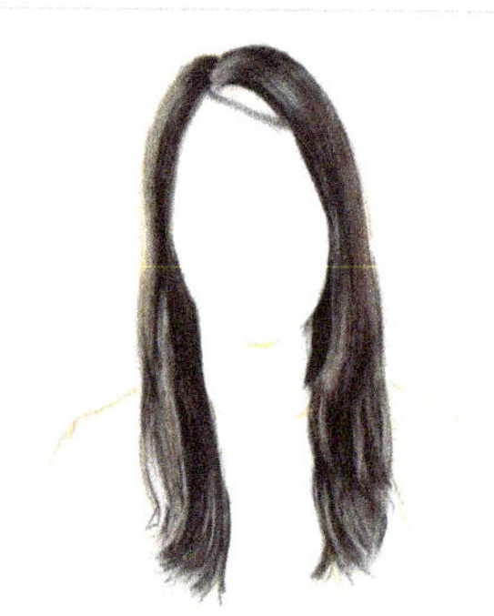

Generally block in the direction of the hair using rough marks of vine charcoal and raw umber.

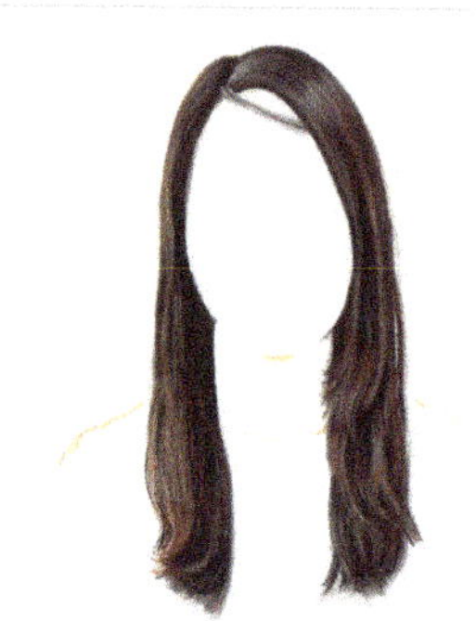

Continue to render the volume of the hair paying attention to the overal volume and introducing different browns mixed with charcoal.

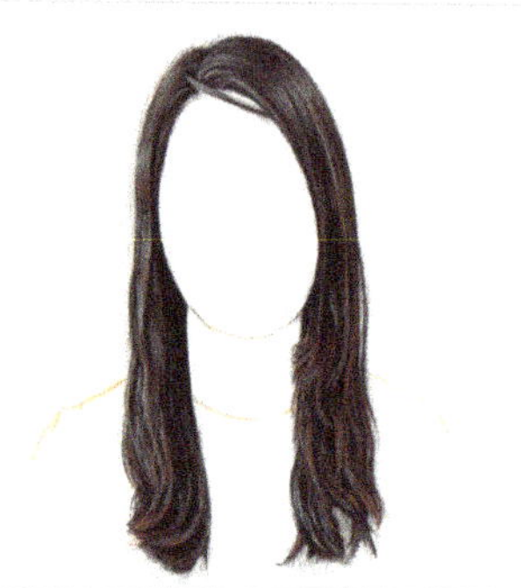

Soften your lines by blending and shading, then render hair lines using the sharp edge of an eraser. Use some yellows and greens to create the illusion of dyed hair.

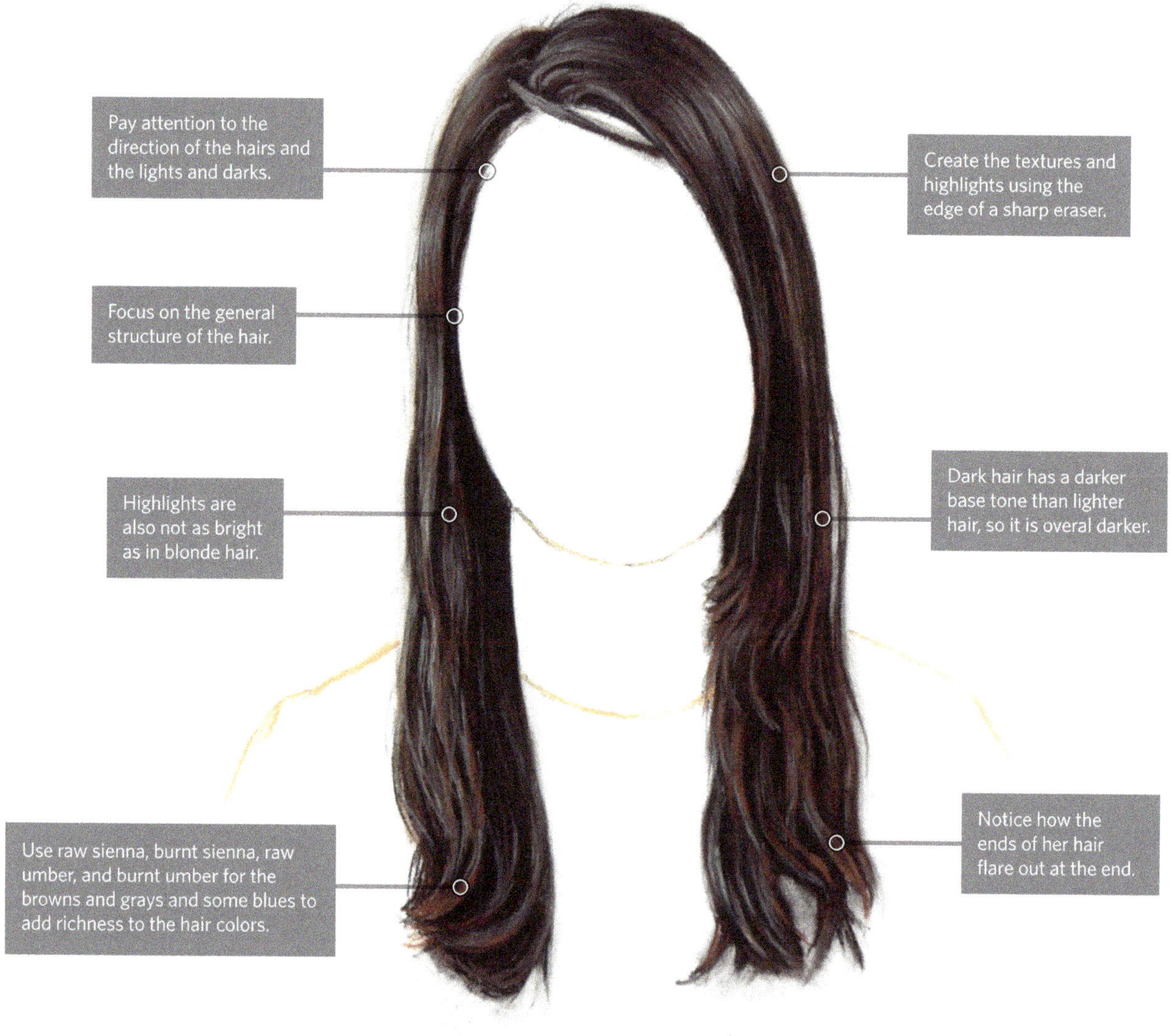

Pay attention to the direction of the hairs and the lights and darks.

Create the textures and highlights using the edge of a sharp eraser.

Focus on the general structure of the hair.

Highlights are also not as bright as in blonde hair.

Dark hair has a darker base tone than lighter hair, so it is overal darker.

Use raw sienna, burnt sienna, raw umber, and burnt umber for the browns and grays and some blues to add richness to the hair colors.

Notice how the ends of her hair flare out at the end.

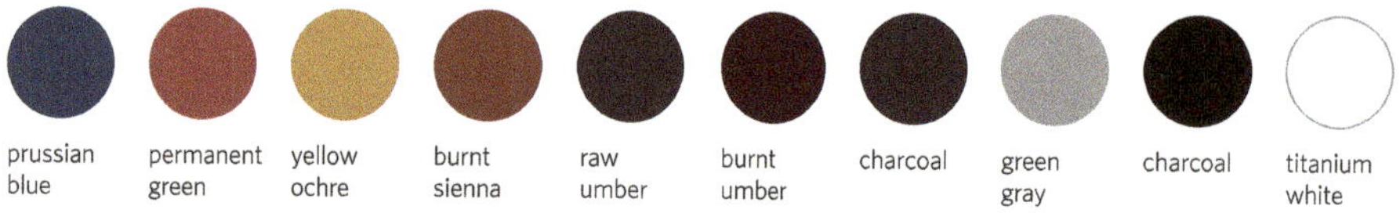

prussian blue · permanent green · yellow ochre · burnt sienna · raw umber · burnt umber · charcoal · green gray · charcoal · titanium white

Now try drawing the long dark straight hair in pastel yourself.

Dark hair contains many brown and red tones. Use these colors to help create volume. Use white sparingly and only in your highlights as white can make your colors chalky and less rich. Remember to layer your colors to create a richer tone in your hair.

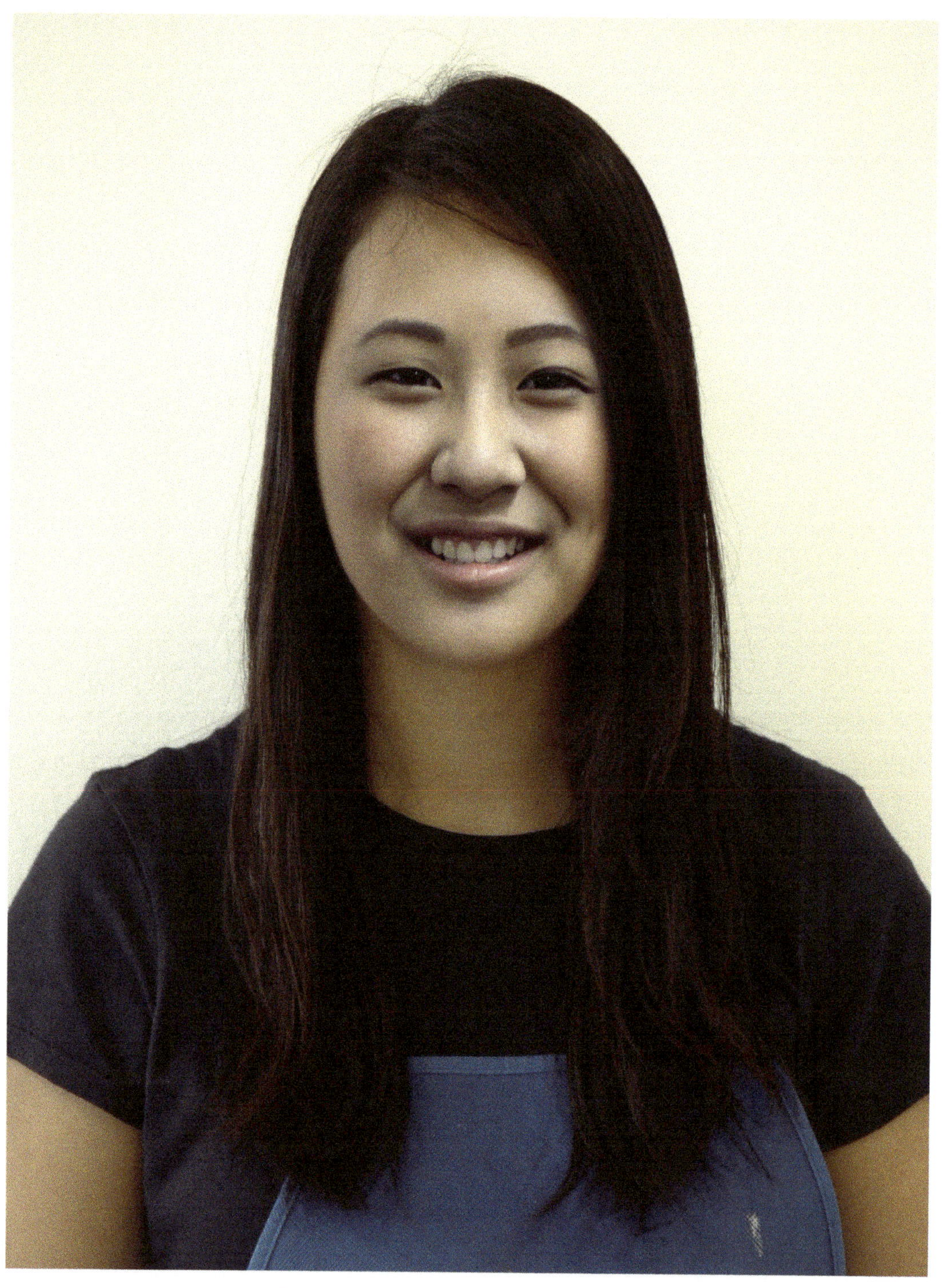

Now try drawing the long dark straight hair in pastel yourself without the grid.

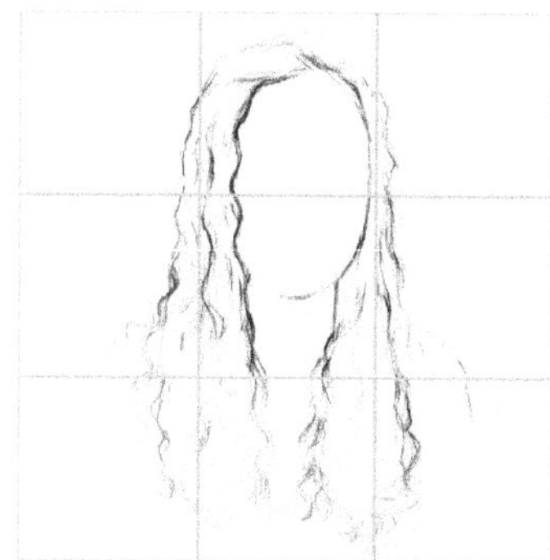

Begin by creating a general outline of the hair and face using vine charcoal

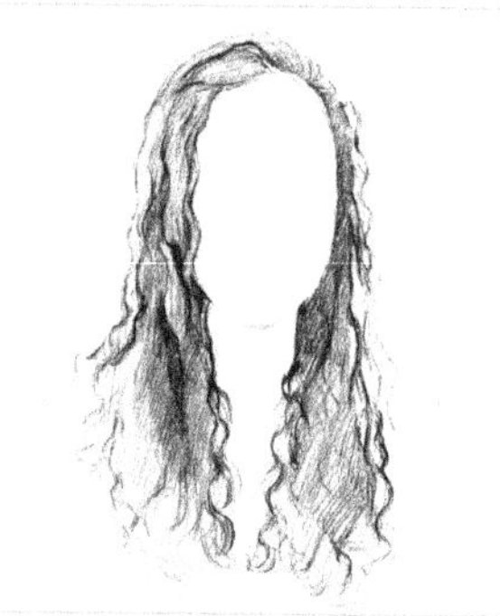

Generally block in the direction of the hair using rough marks.

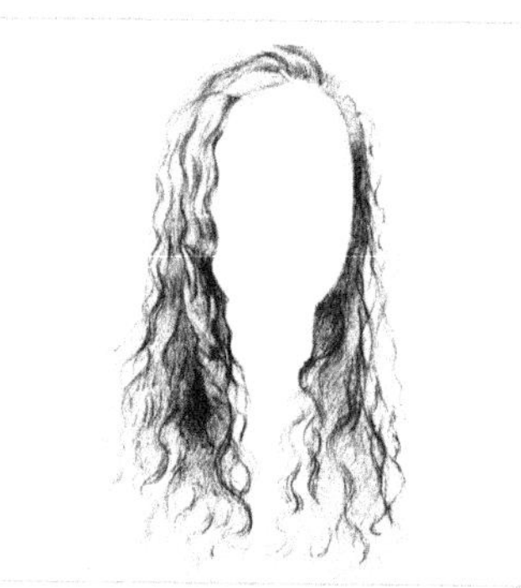

Continue to render the volume of the hair paying attention to the overal volume and introducing compressed charcoal.

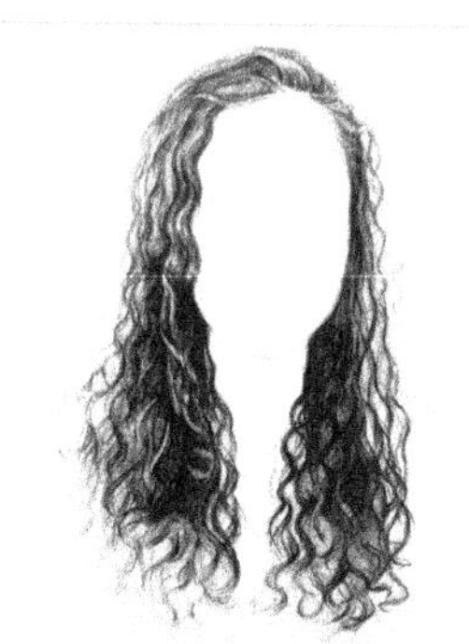

Soften your lines by blending and shading, then render hair lines using the sharp edge of an eraser.

Notice how the hair starts out only wavy and gets curlier at the bottom.

Pay attention to the directions of the hair and how the curls act.

Pay attention to the general areas of light and dark.

At the end, use the sharp edge of an eraser to create highlights.

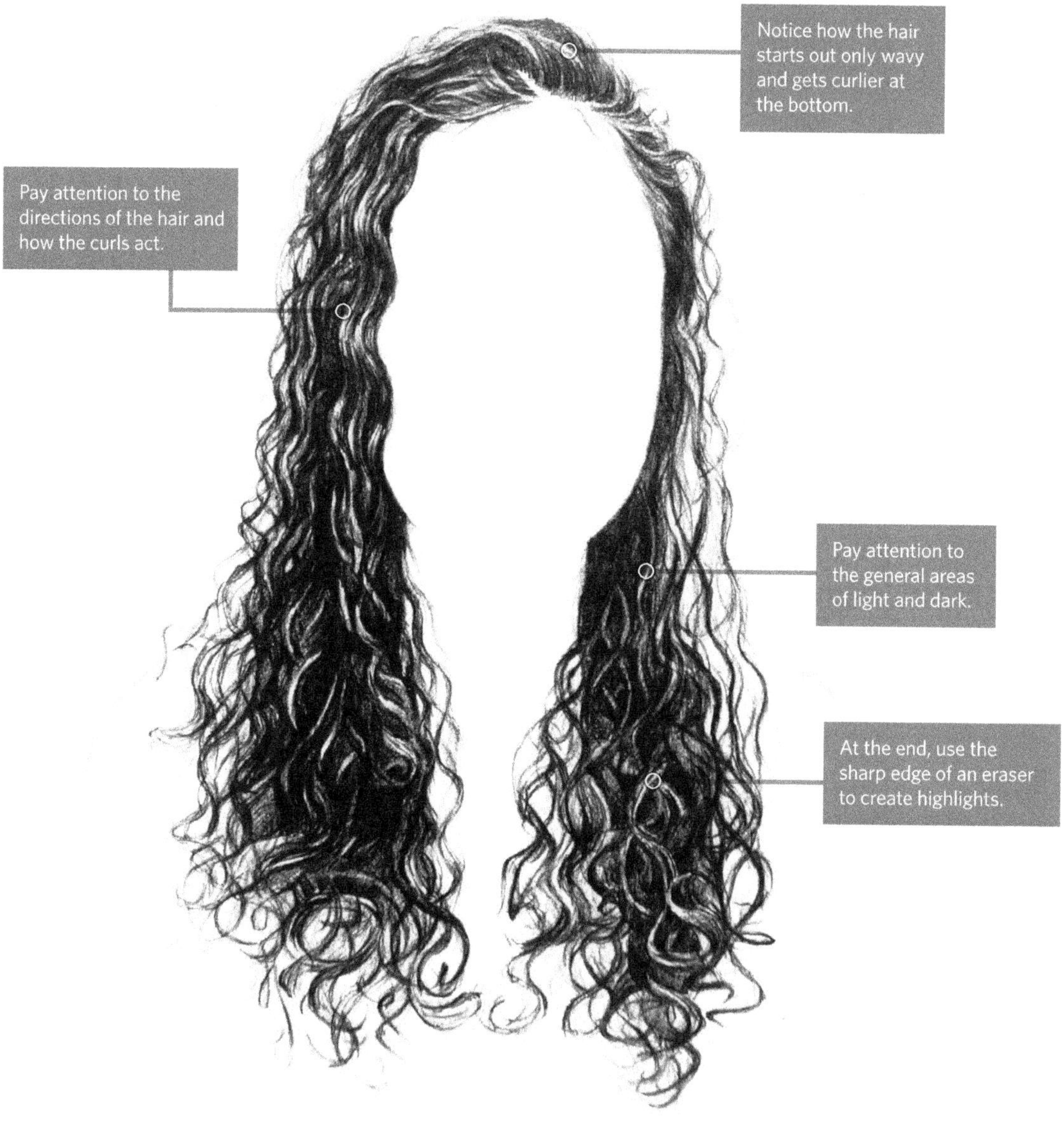

Now try drawing the long dark curly hair in pencil yourself.

Curly hair may look more complicated, but it is, again, a matter of tracing the way the hair curls. First block out the general highlights and shadows of the hair. Then, you can start laying out some of the more prominent locks of hair. Keep the curls uniform in size and add some stray curls.

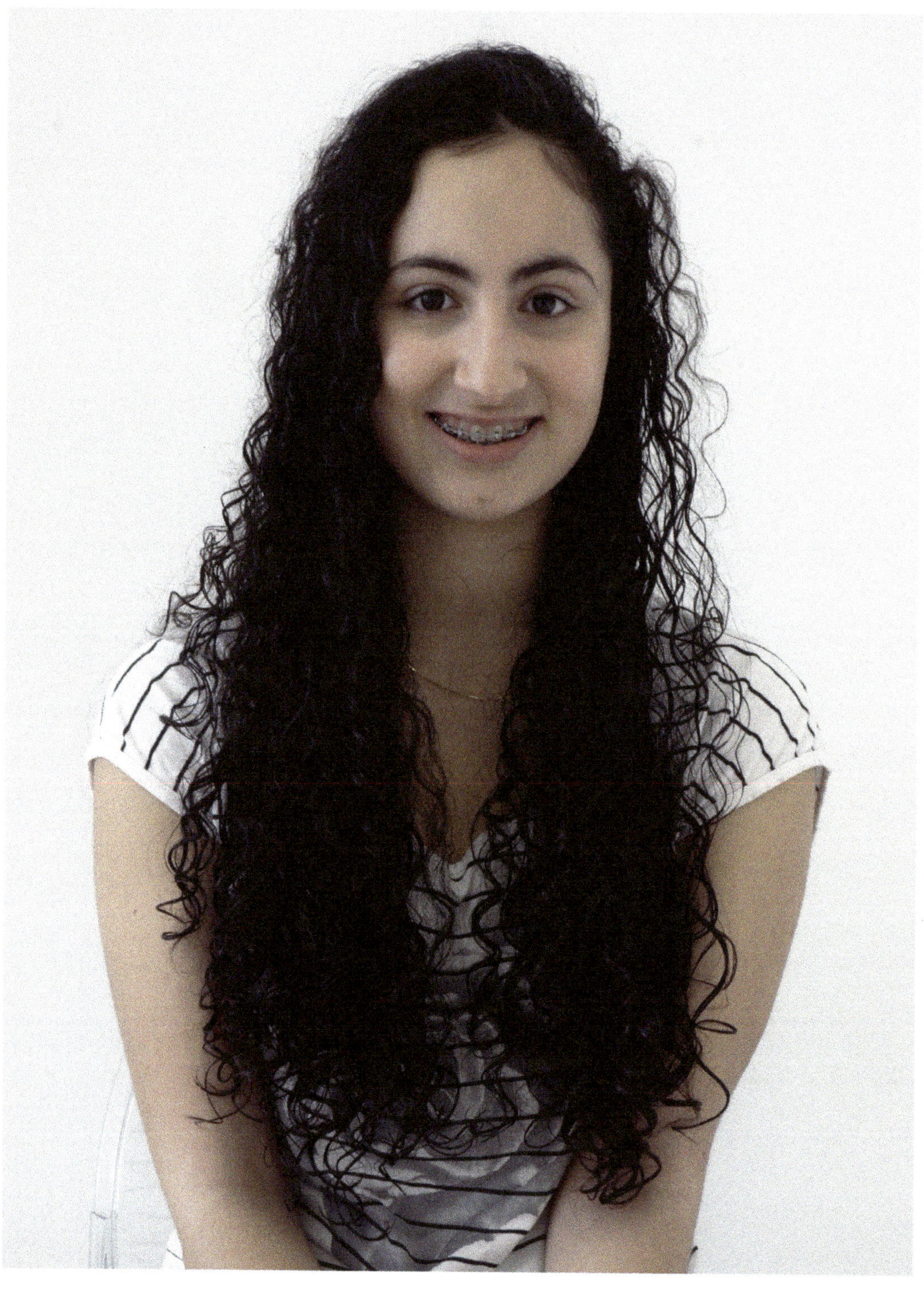

Now try drawing the long dark curly hair in pencil yourself without the grid.

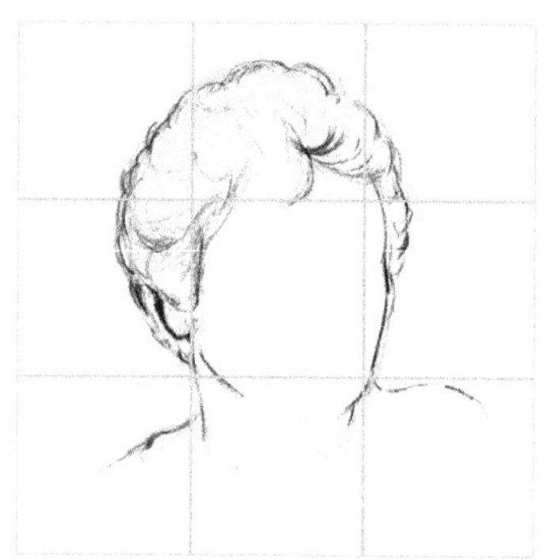

Begin by creating a general outline of the hair and face using vine charcoal.

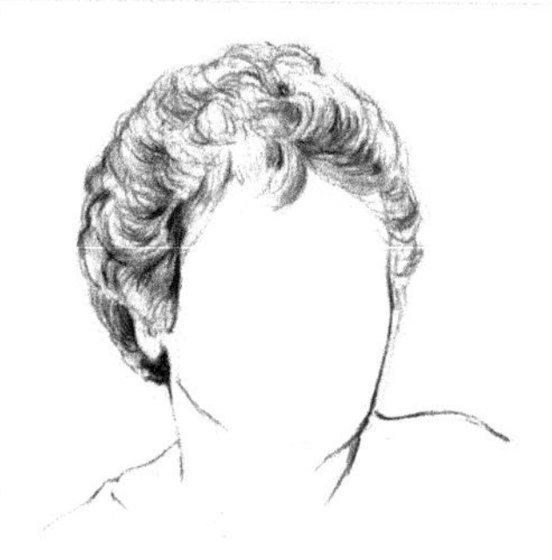

Generally block in the direction of the hair using rough marks.

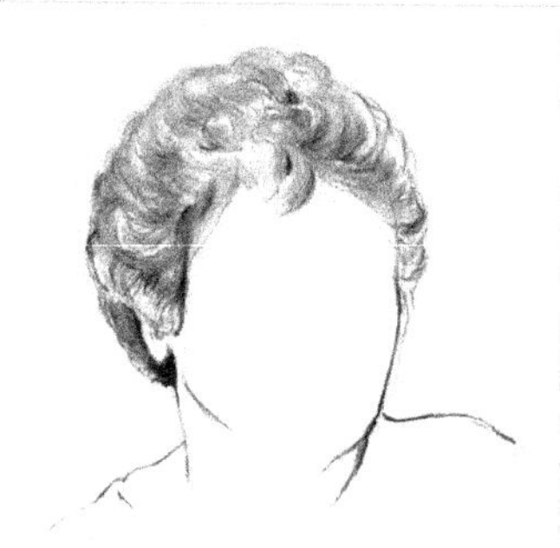

Continue to render the volume of the hair paying attention to the overal volume and introducing compressed charcoal.

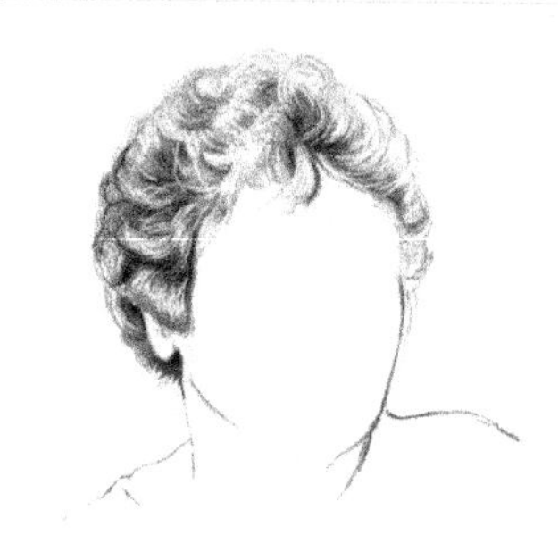

Soften your lines by blending and shading, then render hair lines using the sharp edge of an eraser.

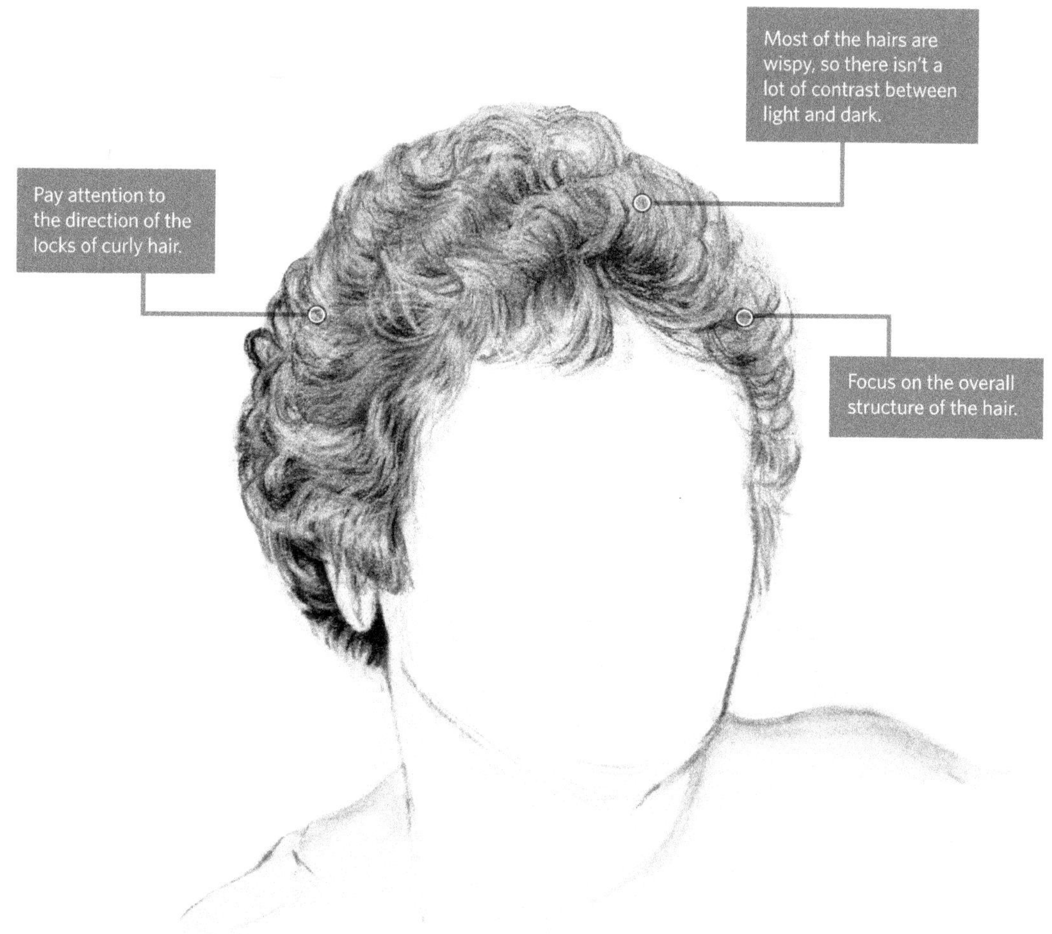

Now try drawing the elder woman's hair in charcoal yourself.

Again, following the direction of the curls is important to creating a realistic looking hairstyle. Focus on adding the shadows and midtones to the curls, for light grey hair, there is less shadow and more midtone. Then you can create texture by erasing in your highlights as well as darken the shadows.

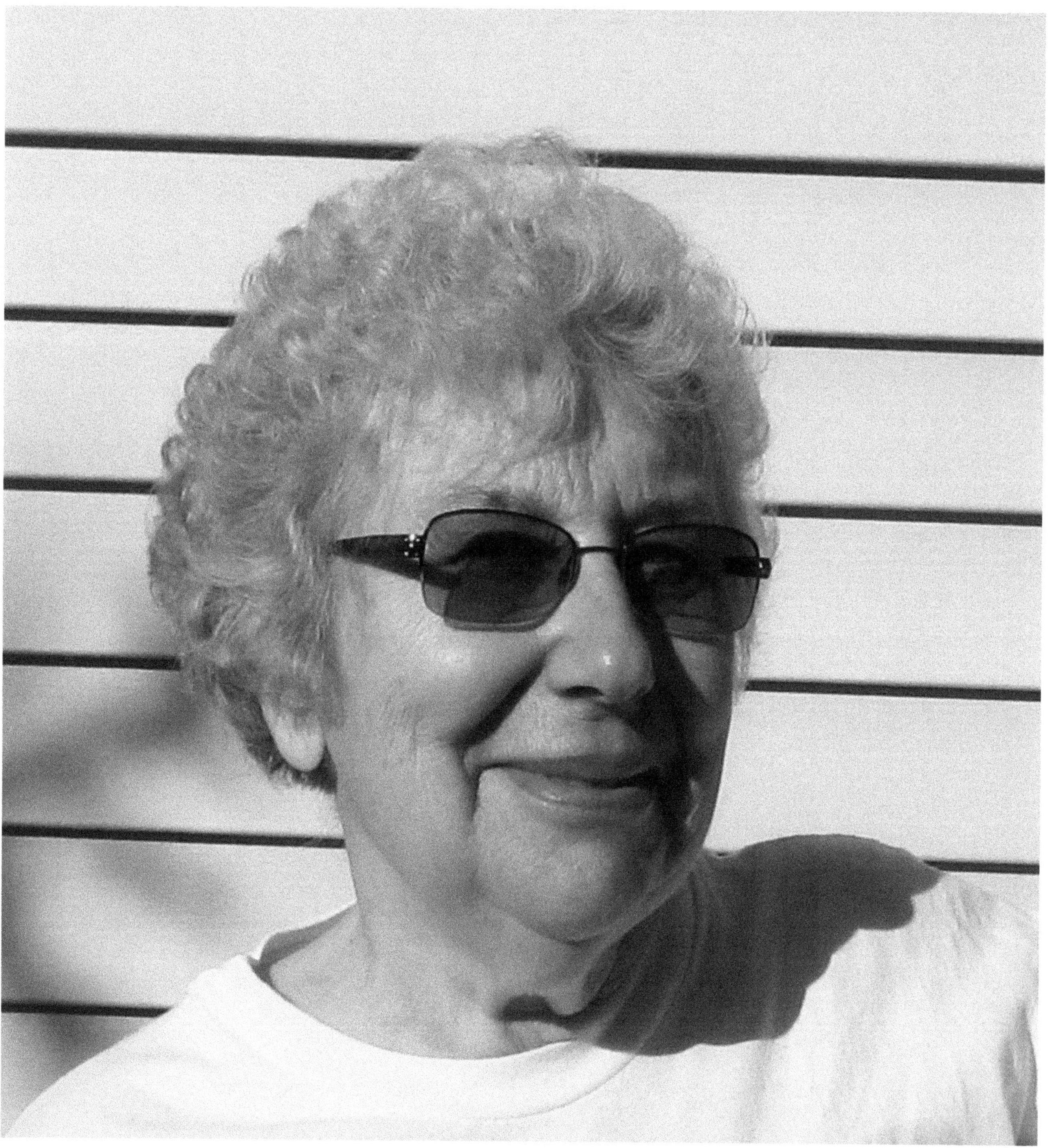

Now try drawing the elder woman hair in charcoal yourself without the grid.

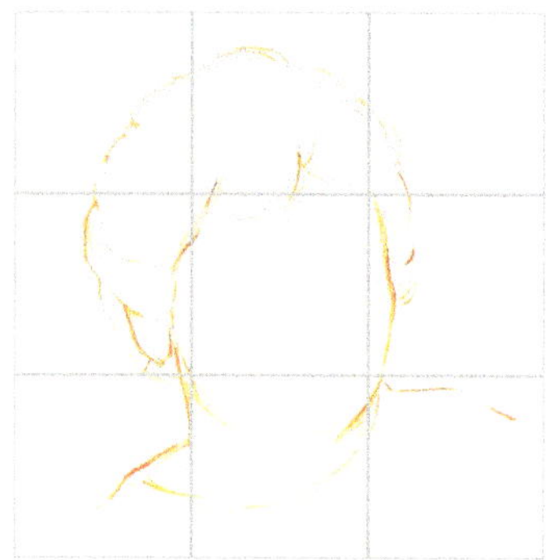

Begin by creating a general outline of the hair and face using a light brown pastel, such as raw sienna.

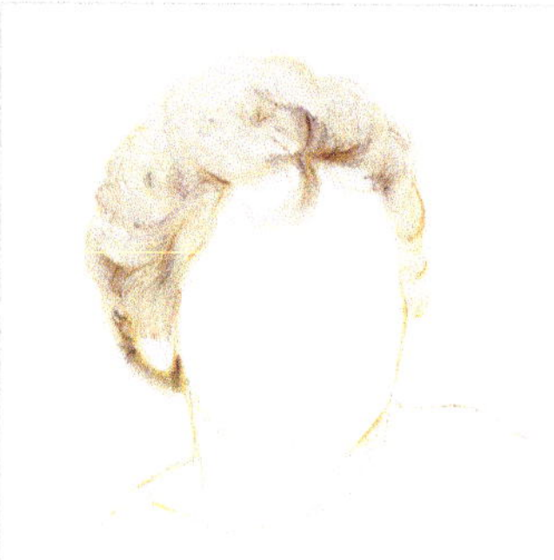

Generally block in the direction of the hair using rough marks of grays, yellow ochre, and raw sienna.

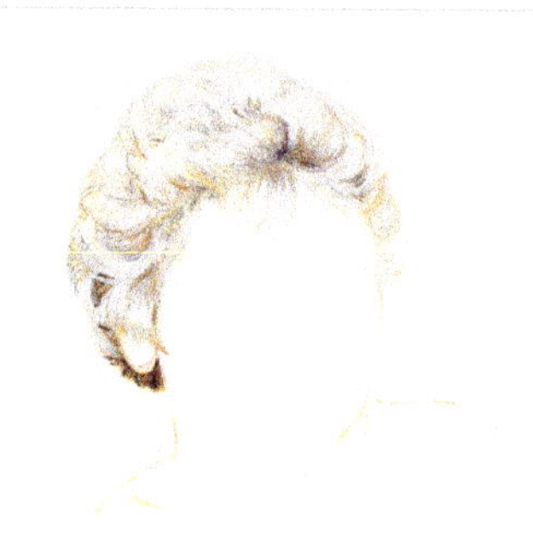

Continue to render the volume of the hair paying attention to the overal volume and introducing different browns mixed with a little bit of vine charcoal.

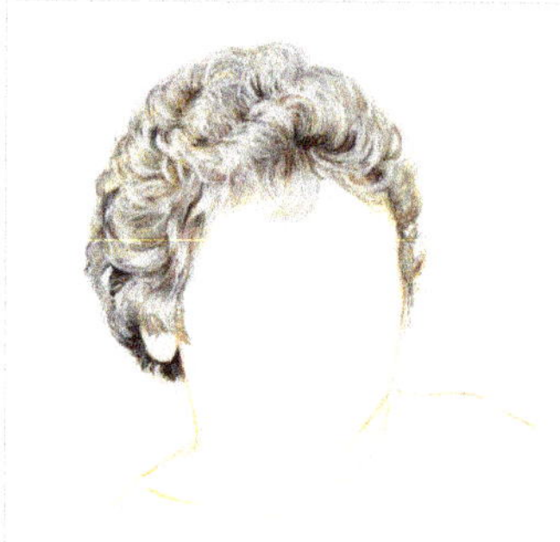

Soften your lines by blending and shading, then render hair lines using the sharp edge of an eraser. Use some yellows and dark grays to create the illusion of volumous curls.

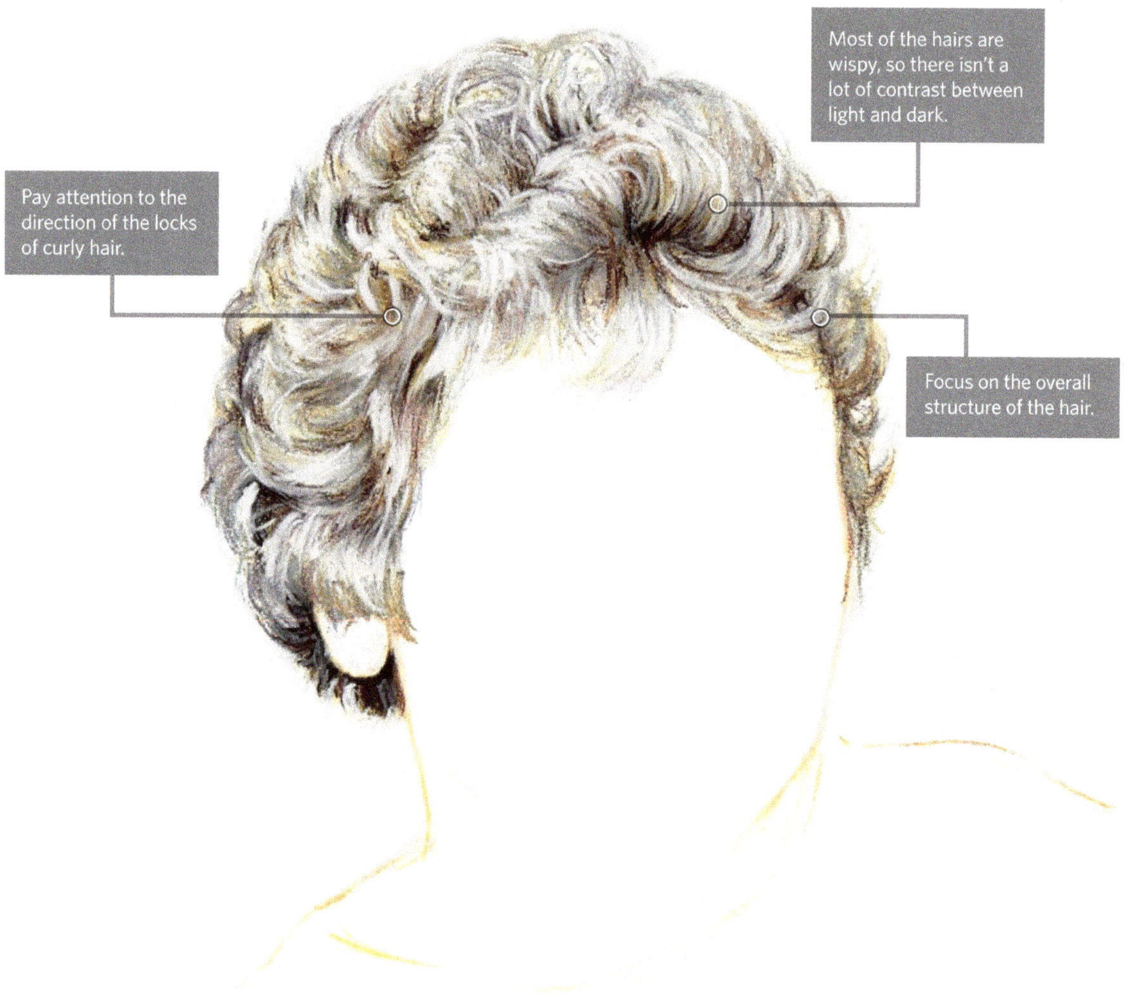

Most of the hairs are wispy, so there isn't a lot of contrast between light and dark.

Pay attention to the direction of the locks of curly hair.

Focus on the overall structure of the hair.

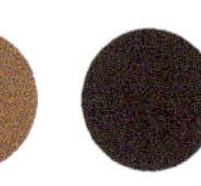
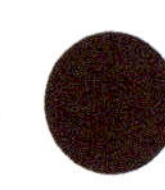
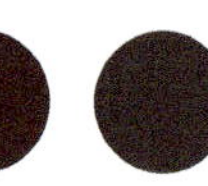
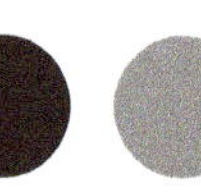

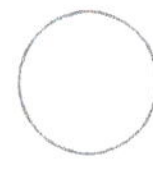

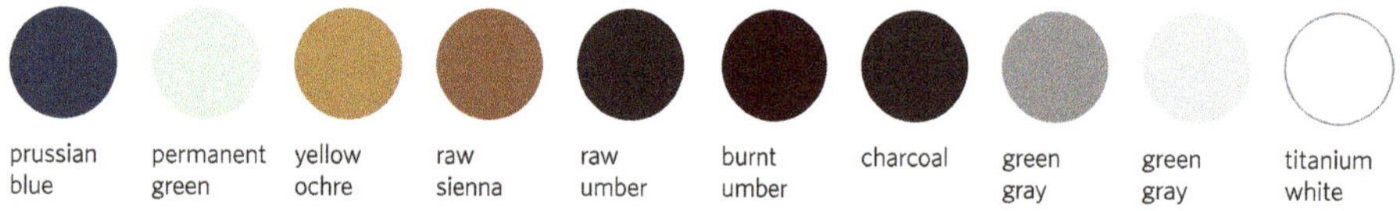

prussian blue · permanent green · yellow ochre · raw sienna · raw umber · burnt umber · charcoal · green gray · green gray · titanium white

Now try drawing the elder woman's hair in pastel yourself.

This hair has a warmer tone to it, so start with warm colors for blocking in your values. Start adding cooler tones into your highlights and adding darker values. Remember keep the shape of the curls in mind as well as the volume of the head for shading.

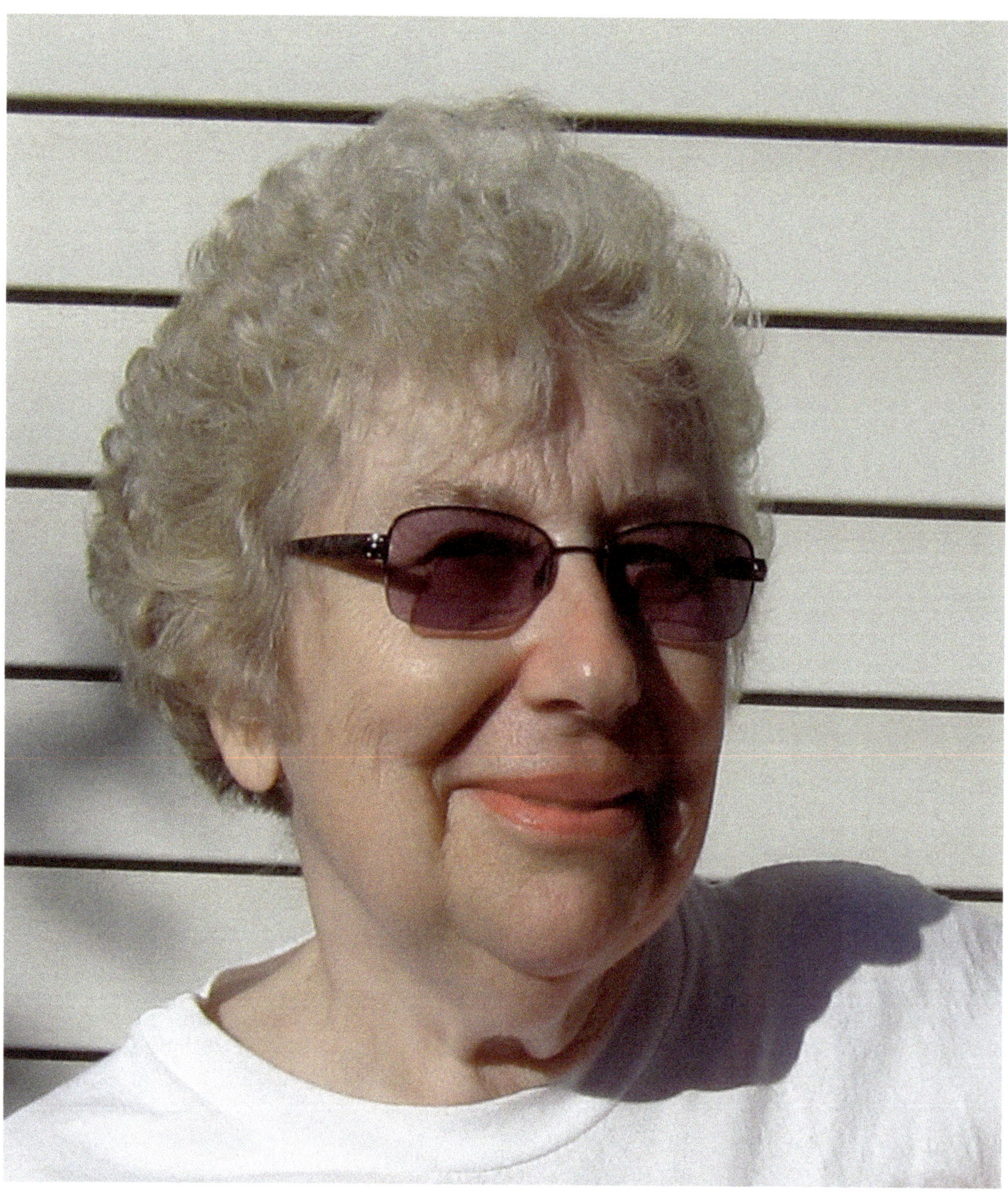

Now try painting the elder lady yourself without the grid.

ABOUT OOGIE HAUS

Oogie Haus is an art foundation unique for its diverse artistic endeavors, including an emphasis in art education, art & design internship opportunities, and volunteer outreach programs. There have been several book publications as well, such as "Art College Admissions," an insightful guideline for students applying to art schools.

Besides being an educational resource, Oogie Haus functions dually as an art gallery and art dealership. Through its research, it seeks to contribute a bigger network for local and international artists simultaneously curating its unique voice in todays art world. For more information please visit www.oogiehaus.com

ABOUT THE AUTHOR

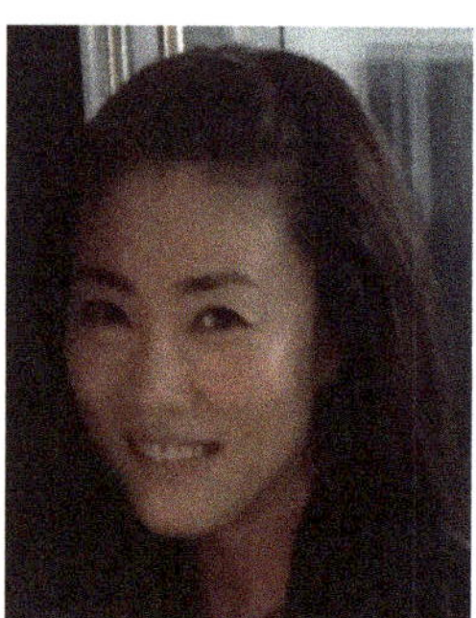

WOOK CHOI is an accomplished art dealer, education columnist, author, art educator, art gallerist, and art portfolio consultant who has guided over a thousand students to college admissions and scholarship success during the course of her 31-year teaching career.
She has received widespread recognition for her teaching methods from Mayor Michael Bloomberg; former First Lady Laura Bush; the New York Commissioner of Education, Richard P. Mills; US Congress member, Jerrold Nadler; the Alliance for Young Artists; YoungArts; and the Marie Walsh Sharpe Foundation. For more information, please visit www.wookchoi.com.

CHECK OUT SOME OF OUR OTHER BOOKS

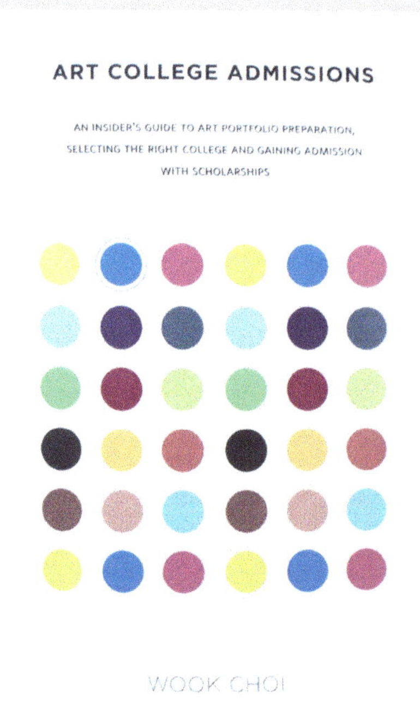

ART COLLEGE ADMISSIONS

An insider's guide to portfolio preparation, selecting the right college and gaining admission with scholarships.
In the first half of this book, you'll learn how vital a role art plays in the success of businesses today, what admissions committees at top art colleges really look for when deciding who to admit, and essential tips for developing award-winning art portfolio pieces. In the second half, you'll learn about the distinct advantages and histories of the most highly-ranked and popular art colleges in the Northeast, specific and actionable tips for getting into each school, and any changes these schools have made to their admissions criteria in recent years.

YOU CAN CONTINUE TO DEVELOP YOUR ARTISTIC SKILLS IN DIFFERENT MEDIA!

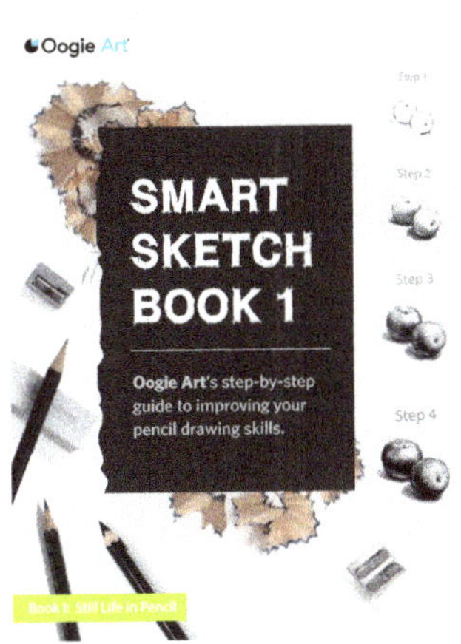

SMART SKETCHBOOK 1:
Still Life in Pencil

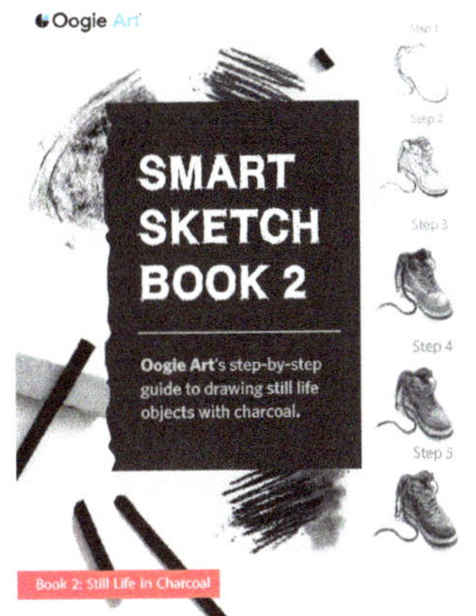

SMART SKETCHBOOK 2:
Still Life in Charcoal

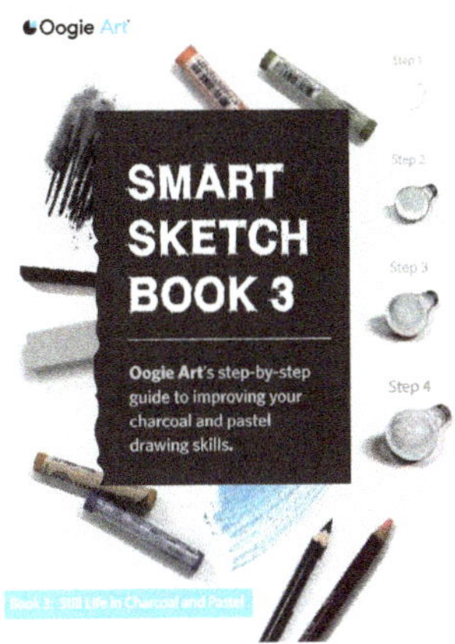

SMART SKETCHBOOK 3:
Still Life in Charcoal and Pastel

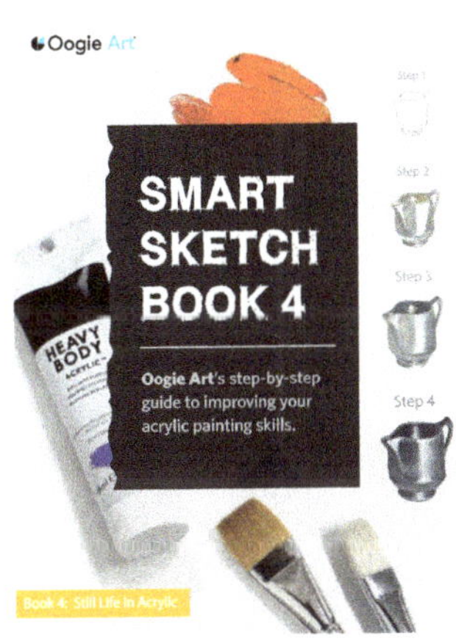

SMART SKETCHBOOK 4:
Still Life in Acrylic

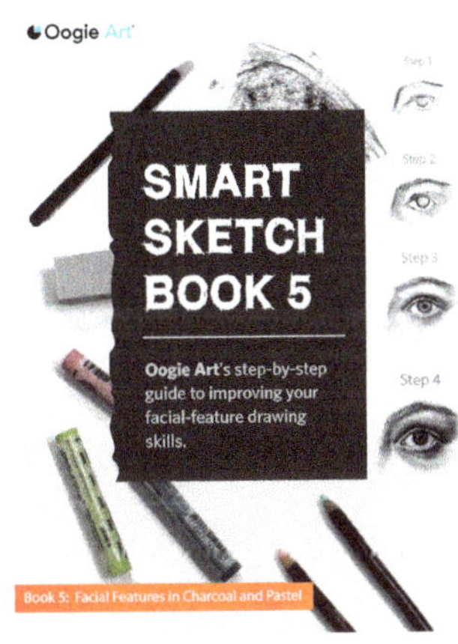

SMART SKETCHBOOK 5:
Facial Features in Charcoal and Pastel

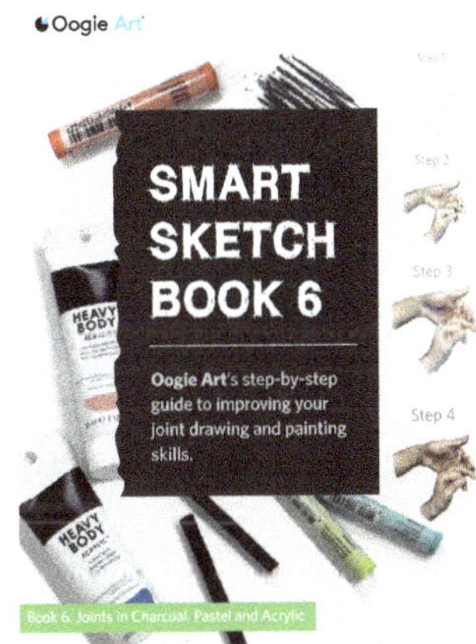

SMART SKETCHBOOK 6:
Joints in Charcoal, Pastel and Acrylic

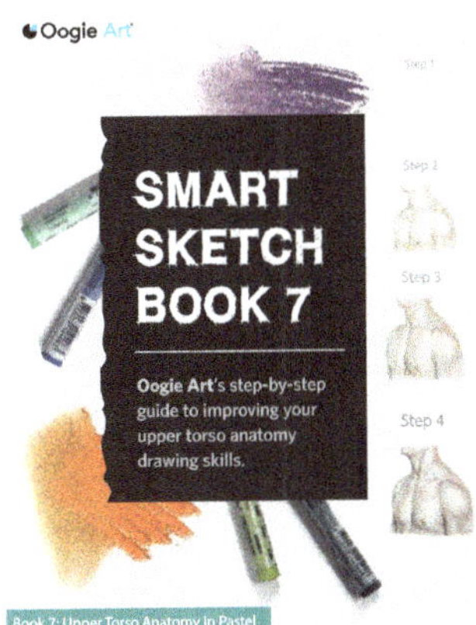

SMART SKETCHBOOK 7:
Upper Torso Anatomy in Pastel

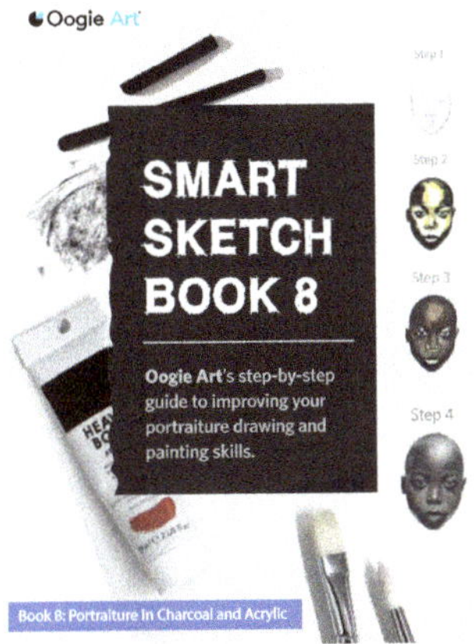

SMART SKETCHBOOK 8:
Portraiture in Charcoal and Acrylic

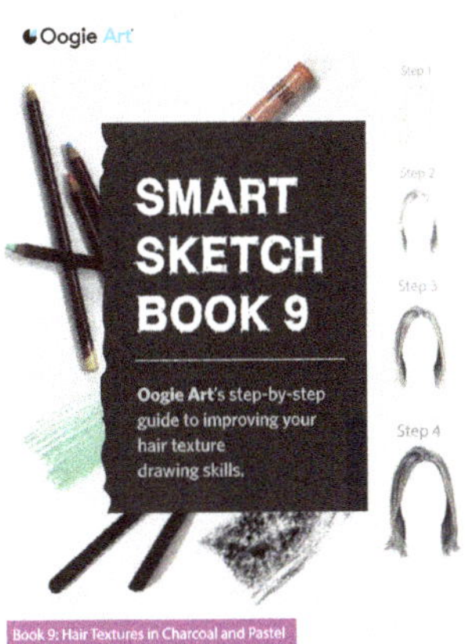

SMART SKETCHBOOK 9:
Hair Textures in Charcoal and Pastel

www.ingramcontent.com/pod-product-compliance
Ingram Content Group UK Ltd.
Pitfield, Milton Keynes, MK11 3LW, UK
UKHW062010290726
14090UKWH00022B/1487

9 780996 821605